Dancing with Loneliness

José María R. Olaizola SJ

Published by Messenger Publications, 2023

Copyright © José María R. Olaizola SJ, 2023

The right of José María R. Olaizola SJ to be identified as the author of the Work has been asserted by him in accordance with the Copyright and Related Rights Act, 2000.

The material in this publication is protected by copyright law. Except as may be permitted by law, no part of the material may be reproduced (including by storage in a retrieval system) or transmitted in any form or by any means, adapted, rented or lent without the written permission of the copyright owners. Applications for permissions should be addressed to the publisher.

ISBN: 978 1 788126 24 3

Designed by Messenger Publications Design Department
Typeset in Garamond Premier Pro
Printed by: Hussar Books

Messenger Publications,
37 Leeson Place, Dublin D02 E5V0
www.messenger.ie

Contents

Foreword by Brian Grogan SJ 5
Introduction 9

Part One: Loneliness, That Untimely Lover
1. The Human Archipelago 14
2. Anything for a Cuddle 18
3. The Signs of Loneliness 20

Part Two: Reasons for Loneliness
4. A Few Personal Reasons 33
5. Is the Media to Blame? Communication Lockdown 46
6. Existential Reasons for Loneliness:
Three Great Contemporary Wounds 56

Part Three: Tango for One
7. 'Kid, Make Your Mind Up. You Can't Have It All.' 72
8. The Tango of Expectation 76
9. What about Me? Selfies or Snapshots 80
10. Feel the Fear 84
11. You're Magnificent 88
12. Someone Else's Shoes: Judgement and Prejudices 94
13. You Need to Start Taking Yourself Seriously 99
14. Dancing with Death 104

Part Four: Encounters

15. My Tribe 110

16. Your People 114

17. Dancing Alone 119

18. The Interior Life: Is There Anyone out There? 125

Conclusion

Two Final Images: Battle Scars and Borders 130

Foreword by Brian Grogan SJ

When I picked up *Dancing with Loneliness*, I expected a book which would make for very sober reading. But this book sparkles, and the word 'dancing' in the title is a key element. The quality of dance in the author's style brings hope and consolation. It's not a systematic exposition of loneliness, rather it moves along rapidly, with points of interest on every page. Anticipation builds up and is not disappointed. Olaizola is perceptive, imaginative and down-to-earth, and he conveys his wisdom through literature, poetry, cinema and personal anecdotes.

There is something in these pages for everyone, whether younger, older, believer or agnostic. All you need is to allow your imagination to help you to explore the world the author paints. He works with an expansive canvas, and readers who reflect on their personal experiences of being lonely will find the pages illuminating. I discovered myself pondering more deeply my own times of loneliness and the loneliness within the lives of those I have lived with: I thought back to what my parents experienced when I left the family home to join the Jesuits, and how my brother coped with the tragic death of his wife and his later battle with cancer.

The author distinguishes a healthy solitude and aloneness from an insidious loneliness, which he terms 'vicious' because it is destructive. Rather than having us avoid the pain and isolation within human existence, he sees aloneness itself as a lifetime travelling companion, an essential element in human development. Aloneness becomes unhealthy only when it goes on too long and when needed support is missing. Even infants experience aloneness from being left alone, while children have to adapt to the strains and gaps within family life. Teenagers are caught between the desire for independence while still depending on authority. With the pressure of social media comes the need to shine in front of others, and loneliness – often desperate – takes over if one cannot fit into the group.

Moving along, the young adult is faced with decisions about study, work, career, relationships, places to live, finance, and these have to be made alone. As the years move on comes the jolting discovery that no one else can live your life for you. With partnering and children a carefree existence ends, responsibilities take over and routine can set in. Married life has its tedium; one can be stuck in an unsatisfying relationship, or unable to have children, or if you do have kids you may find it difficult to get through to them. 'Do my kids love me still? Does my partner?' Loneliness can pervade a whole life, as when you never meet that special person who would make you feel that you are the centre of the universe.

With seniority, health issues arise, energy diminishes, and there are fewer friends. With retirement may come inactivity. Life still has plenty to offer, but you don't know how to fill your days well, and you feel you're a bother, useless, ignored. Mortality impinges: peers die and leave a gaping rent in your social life; questions arise about the meaning of life, its limits, and the puzzle of life beyond death.

Olaizola bravely reviews his own celibate life in terms of loneliness. When contemplating the step of becoming a Jesuit he imagined that no life could be lonelier than that of a celibate. Would his future entail loving everything and everyone, or would he turn into a crabby, taciturn bachelor, morosely reflecting on paths unchosen? Happily the life he chose led to his heart and mind being full of people he is very fond of. He has discovered that loneliness exists in every life. The desire for physical intimacy does not disappear, 'but today I sense that it is sometimes far lonelier to share a bed with your lifelong partner when you are separated by a wall of silence . . . than it is to sleep alone'.

Having caught our attention and illuminated how times of healthy loneliness can be embraced as a creative emptiness within which something new and life-giving can develop, he zooms in on what he terms 'vicious' loneliness, which is destructive and does not carry the seed of new growth. It is painful and unwanted, 'a tortuous tango', but he encourages us to trust that despite our faltering steps we can extricate ourselves from it. With this promise he faces into the tangled world of relationships.

A recent report states that Eastern European countries are among the ones with the highest prevalence of loneliness in Europe. Some sociologists even refer to our time as 'the lonely century' and speak of 'an epidemic of loneliness'. Such loneliness can originate in many ways. Many older people are living alone, not by choice but because family supports have crumbled. Twenty years ago the Polish sociologist Zygmunt Bauman coined the term 'liquid society' to describe how diffuse and fluid once-solid social structures have become. People move around and live very different lives, so it is now harder for them to focus on what they have in common.

Olaizola emphasises that younger people can be trapped in the negative side of social media: they can feel left out of the group and wonder why everything seems to go better for 'the others' who seem fulfilled, beautiful, always on a high; no grey days or weeks of dull routine. Loneliness ensues. Casual relationships do not satisfy the desire to know and be known, to share inner emotions, even if dark, and still be respected. He quotes Bruckner: 'When feeling evaporates, nothing's left'. To have 'friends' and 'followers' makes one 'popular', but the virtual world may be a refuge for the lonely. The effort to be liked can't be sustained forever. We want the illusion of a relationship but not the real thing. Digital platforms, he says, have more than a few bullying barbarians, who push and shove, love and hate each other, know and persecute each other.

Younger people need help to discover that it is up to them to decide what to make of themselves. Then they begin to step away from the drifters. To paraphrase the late philosopher-theologian Bernard Lonergan, writing more than forty years ago, drifters are those who have not yet found themselves; they are content to do what everyone else is doing. They have not yet developed minds of their own, so they think and say what everyone else is thinking and saying.

Olaizola highlights gospel characters who are struggling with loneliness: Martha is alienated from her sister Mary because she is left to do all the serving alone; Jesus hints that she may be missing out on something more important. The man forgiven a huge debt who can't see that he should forgive his fellow-servant who owes a small sum is caught in the solitude of the selfie and thinks, 'I alone matter!' The younger son in the parable, who takes all he can from his father, comes to himself in his isolation and misery and sees that his only way forward is to ask his father for mercy. The wounded traveller is saved by the out-going love of the good Samaritan. Peter denies his Lord but is restored through repentant love.

The book closes with short reflections on our encounters with the divine. Ordinary life can be the setting for meeting God because the events of our lives are signs pointing to the beyond. Next, we need to read the Bible as addressed personally to ourselves: in this way our relationship with God becomes alive. Further, we can learn to see the sacraments as celebrating hope, new beginnings, community, love, forgiveness, and finally, no matter what way we pray, we are reaching out to God.

Each of us is magnificent, the author says, and we are already caught up into a web of loving relationships with God and all others. All our lives are worth telling. We need not live like ghosts, barely interacting with the real world. We can tango alone or together, and this book teaches us the steps!

Introduction

Loneliness is one of the most universal of all human experiences, a singular companion on our life journey. It is quite a complex feeling. Sometimes it brings peace, at other times it's overwhelming: we just don't know what to do with the feelings stirring inside us. At times, we all feel alone. That doesn't necessarily mean that we feel low. Indeed, sometimes we seek solitude and even long to be alone. At these times, an absence of close ties, having some silence and a bit of space from other people is peaceful rather than threatening or oppressive. At other times, loneliness is not so welcome. It can be a painful experience that we neither want nor quite know how to handle.

Who hasn't at some point experienced the pain of loneliness? When it's unwanted, and unexpected – you are both upset and dejected. You long for someone else to be there for you, to say a friendly word, give you a reassuring embrace, or offer a shoulder to cry on. This type of loneliness reflects insecurities about your own self-worth, guilt over poor decision-making you don't dare reveal to others, and bouts of ridiculous fears you keep to yourself. When you feel like this, you begin to crave meals with a friend, or the consolation of sharing a joke, a consoling hug, or even just a chat with someone who really cares for you. This type of loneliness is exasperating – as when you stare for hours at your email inbox or social media waiting for a message, a text, a call or reply that just never comes. It can even pitch up when you're surrounded by people, without a moment for yourself, yet you feel as though you're in an empty space, overwhelmed by a vast, endless desert-like silence. When this takes over, you may end up feeling bereft and ashamed. You feel like an orphan, deprived of companions. You feel shame because your solitude feels as though it is certifying an utter failure to connect with others. 'There must be something wrong with me. That's why I'm alone,' is your unjust, self-flagellating conclusion. Then it begins, the endless self-analysis: you minutely dissect your flaws, getting angry with the world, yourself and God. You try to hide your loneliness, masking it with indifference. You put up a front, shrug your shoulders and disguise your frustration with a mask of humour, coldness or business. You take refuge in empty consolations that fill your time and sense of emptiness. But the loneliness is still there, lurking, getting to you, occasionally rattling your very foundation.

This kind of loneliness, which can be really hard to cope with, is sometimes unavoidable. But we can learn to cope with it. It's neither the end of the world nor a sign of failure, just one particular mood in our emotional spectrum. You might struggle to believe this, but the truth is we all experience loneliness, albeit in different, highly individual ways.

Every human being longs for profound connection with others, for closeness, intimacy and belonging. To be human means being in relationship with others. Our relationships define and sustain us. No one can truly say who they are without naming their social networks, their loved ones and friends. What makes us human are our relationships – the fact that we are friends, parents, teachers, lovers, sons and daughters, employers, disciples, doctors, patients, members of a community, colleagues, enemies or in a couple. Obviously, not all our relationships have the same significance or meaning. Nor will they all fill our loneliness in exactly the same way. The more secondary or less meaningful a relationship is, the less it will influence this profound and private experience. Some relationships simply don't fulfil our need for connection and belonging. Others do. Perhaps they're fewer in number, but most of us have a few special friends or relations whose names are close to our hearts.

Loneliness and connection are not enemies, but two facets of everyone's life. We just need to get to know them. That's especially true of loneliness, so that, far from being oppressive or a threat, it can become an opportunity or a learning point. Through loneliness we can learn to bond with ourselves and with others. Far from consuming our self-esteem or wearing us out, aloneness can be an ally in the exciting and complicated battles of life. All we need to do is discern the heart song of loneliness, so that we can learn how to guide our emotions to cope with it. This heart song consists of our acceptance and desire, our lucidity

Introduction

and awareness, our memory and hope, our faith and inner turmoil. All of that is in this book: loneliness and connection, silence and music.

Personally, I find the image of a dance a fitting metaphor for expressing the many ways in which we engage with each other. That's why I have chosen this metaphor to guide us through the book. In my mind, the world is filled with the music in our hearts. Everyone has a different song. Once we have learned to discern these unique melodies, they help us to move or interact with each other in a way that is new, original, alternative. This internal soundtrack invites us to transform our external interactions or moves into a dance. Sometimes it soothes us. At other times it invigorates. Sometimes we move alone, at others times we dance in company.

At the 2008 Oscars, the award for best soundtrack went to Italian conductor Dario Marianelli for his brilliant composition for the film *Atonement*.[1] Probably his greatest stroke of genius, which led to Marianelli winning other major awards that season, was his decision to overlay the sound of the piano with the clatter of a typewriter in the film's overture. Briony, the main character, is a young girl who is writing her first play. The frenzy of the typewriter keys against the paper produces an intense, almost anxious sound that reflects Briony's conflicting emotions: her restlessness, her haste, her perfectionism, her demand for attention. From then on, we know this is going to be her heart song or emotional soundtrack, derived from everyday sounds. Likewise, we each have our own heart song framing our personal sounds, our words, silence, rhythm, feelings and connections.

At various stages in this book, I'll refer to music and dance and suggest film scenes to illustrate the points I'm making, as in the paragraph above. Each scene is an extract from a full-length or short film. While not all of them are on the Internet, many are readily available, so wherever possible, I'll include the relevant YouTube link in the footnotes. Watching the films is not essential in order for you to follow my line of thought, but it may offer another way of reading the text, because the

---

1. T. Bevan (producer) and J. Wright (director), *Atonement*, Studio Canal, 2007, http://bit.ly/2vSLxyU.

Introduction

images may enrich my words. If you find it helpful, please don't hesitate to alternate between the text and the video clips.

I don't claim to cover in these pages everything that might be said about loneliness. I'm conscious that to do so is beyond me. Indeed, I'm not sure that even a whole library could do justice to the topic. Nor am I aiming to generalise and create a rule out of what, in many instances, are personal experiences. My only aim is to share some observations that may help you, the reader, to reflect further, applying these observations to your own life, and enriching and completing them with your own memories, experiences and personal journey. Whether you're young or old, I'm positive you can find something to identify with in these experiences. It is my hope that this book may lead you to find a heart song that is meaningful and lasting, both when you are lonely and for your life in general.

Part One

Loneliness, That Untimely Lover

It was the singer Joaquin Sabina who, in one of his best-known songs, expressed this universal sentiment: 'And sometimes lying my head against the shoulder of the Moon, I tell it about that untimely lover called loneliness'. This is a lovely turn of phrase, coupling aloofness with warmth, love with pain, a stolen caress, yearned for and passionate, with the irritation of an unwelcome embrace. Something similar happens to us with loneliness. It haunts us: sometimes as an ally, at other times as an enemy. It inspires us, yet it somehow paralyses us too. Sometimes we want and need to be alone, at other times we hate it, and loneliness creates within us a cry that is all the more deafening because no one else seems to hear it.

The following chapters will attempt to pin down what loneliness is, a sort of clearing of the ground in order to plant the seeds of new ideas. I'll attempt to show that loneliness affects all our lives, but also how it differs for each one of us.

1

The Human Archipelago

The Catholic monk Thomas Merton gave one of his highly popular books an enchanting title: *No Man is an Island*.[2] Five words that become a promise. What hope is concealed in that title! It is undoubtedly a perspective that may help us to make sense of the bonds connecting us to each other, and to God.

No one wants to be an island. The word 'isolated' almost always carries negative connotations: it's applied to the undesirables, the impure, those suffering contagious diseases. In a world built on fame and powerful alliances, the weak are isolated, like pariahs, the condemned or anyone deserving punishment.

How many films about prisons feature an 'isolation cell' as the worst kind of punishment? There, the prisoner's experience of separation from fellow inmates, of confinement, of solitude and silence, is worse than any threat or violence. The convict has to battle with the absence of speech, a prison tougher than isolation in a cell. Also tough is the loneliness. There is no one to share the prisoner's suffering. Remember the epic heroism of Colonel Nicholson (Alec Guinness) in the first part of *The Bridge on the River Kwai*. In truly adverse conditions, he endures imprisonment by the Japanese and eventually triumphs after managing not to succumb to either discouragement or madness. A few years ago, another film, the Argentine *El secreto de sus ojos* (The Secret in Their Eyes), toyed with the idea of isolation as a punishment, suggesting that the

---

2. The title is from a poem by John Donne: 'No man is an island entire of itself; every man / is a piece of the continent, a part of the main; / if a clod be washed away by the sea, Europe / is the less, as well as if a promontory were, as / well as any manner of thy friends or of thine / own were; any man's death diminishes me, / because I am involved in mankind. / And therefore never send to know for whom / the bell tolls; it tolls for thee.'

most refined form of revenge is lifelong solitary imprisonment. The film shows how the guilty party, in a strategy that inexorably leads to his self-destruction, is isolated to deprive him of human contact, conversation or any kind of interaction. In a moving scene, this man, after many years of solitary confinement, pleads with the main character to intercede for him with his captor. 'Please,' he begs, 'ask him to at least speak to me, to say something, anything.' Note that no longer does he ask for freedom. Only that his captor speak to him.[3]

Isolating someone may seem somewhat extreme, a setting up of barriers which, in the long term, leads to solitary confinement. For all of these reasons, when Merton declares that 'no man is an island', his words contain an implicit promise. However alone you may feel, there must be some kind of space, sphere or opening through which you can hold on to others – or to God who is the Other.

Not being an island means having access to significant others, that there's someone nearby with whom you have a shared bond of affection, or love or passion, a rock-solid connection with someone with whom you're able to live, to talk, someone you can love, trust and dance with.

However, we need to oppose Merton's statement. That's not to discredit Merton, who had a deep, brilliant and intuitive knowledge of both the human person and of faith, but instead to complement what he's saying. While agreeing with Merton that no one is an island, it's also fair to say, at the same time, that all of us are like islands. Years ago I wrote a fortnightly column for the weekly Spanish Catholic magazine *Vida Nueva* (New Life). I covered many subjects – society, culture, the Church, topical news items and more perennial topics. Occasionally a reader would comment on what I'd written, sometimes saying they agreed with me, at other times to pick me up on particular points. Receiving such messages was rare, at least until the week I wrote the article below, which was titled 'The Human Archipelago'.

---

3. G. Herrero (producer) and J. Campanella (director), *El secreto de sus ojos*, Haddock Films, 2009, http://bit.ly/2vSHcvt.

Sometimes I feel like we all have something of an island about us. We live in contact with others (perhaps many, perhaps only a few. It all depends: everyone's story is unique). We see each other from a distance (maybe greater, maybe lesser, but a distance all the same). And those people whose lives entwine with ours include everybody we know: our parents, siblings, children, colleagues, neighbours, friends, lovers, bosses, employees, partners, the people who serve us in shops, businesses, etc., or who, we, through our jobs, serve.

Yet however much our paths cross, however much we acknowledge each other and share parts of our life journey, however much we search and sometimes even until we find intimacy, or love, in each one of us, there's a unique place of solitude and depth that no one else will even glimpse. There are so many thoughts, ideas and feelings which we never share with others. So many secrets and hidden desires, hopes, tears and fears. So much of our daily life is hidden and anonymous.

This is one of the most fruitful albeit most painful tensions in life: moving between solitude and togetherness, from distance to encounter, from self-differentiating to unity. And that's exactly how we live, as though we're building a bridge to reach other people, or seeking a ship that allows us to berth even if only briefly in exotic ports; opening up our inner terrain so that others may wade in. We veer between the joy of discovering that others are close to us, and the pain of not possessing them, or of letting them go when the time is right, of respecting their timing, their personal space and their silence.

We are created for connection with others and for communion. I say to all those who are alone, who weep in secret, you whose wounds are muted, whose fears are hidden, you to whom so many doors have closed, and whose affections have been spurned ... I say to you, we cannot give in.

Great was my surprise after this column was published when, over the following weeks, I received more messages than I had ever received for all of my previous articles put together. Very different people wrote to tell me that they identified with my description of the Human Archipelago. They said I could have been talking about them. They said that they too often felt as though they were islands, struggling in their solitary nook, and that the tensions I described could have been an X-ray of some of their own relationships.

I felt like replying that probably, as I was writing that column, I was describing myself, during one of those times when you have to fight your own demons. The truth is that doubtless I had described both my correspondents and myself. I had pinpointed something that is part of the lives of many of us (perhaps occasionally all of our lives): those very human tensions between being close to each other or far apart, or being close to others and being detached, between connection and separation, between physical contact and isolation.

Part One

2

Anything for a Cuddle

Many years ago, while I was a young Jesuit novice, I went on a retreat with my fellow novices. Halfway through the year in early January, we usually made a three-day retreat to renew our vows. It was a chance to renew our motivation a bit, to take a break from daily life and to try to deepen the meaning of our commitment to poverty, chastity and obedience.

One particular day, the Jesuit leading us in prayer spoke of the vow of chastity. He had suggested we look at a few texts on love in the Gospels, and was giving us a few insights on the meaning of the vow. I don't remember his exact words, but they were along the lines of presenting chastity not as a kind of isolation, loneliness or repression, but rather as the sign of an alternative way of loving. His words were beautiful and had real depth. However, having said all this, he paused briefly as if to capture our attention and, when there was an expectant silence, he said: 'Well, now, there's something you need to be aware of: there'll be times in your life where you'd give it all up for a cuddle.'

The silence that followed these words was deathly. We were nearly a hundred young men, most of us in our twenties. A statement like that touched on one of our deepest fears. It's one thing to dive into a lifelong commitment fuelled by daring, passion and the naivety of youth. It's quite another to begin to discover just what 'for ever' really means. If, when I made my vows at twenty, I had assumed that I had a handle on everything and that things were always going to be easy, by the age of twenty-two I was starting to realise that many struggles and dilemmas lay ahead of me. The warning of this fellow Jesuit – who was far older and more experienced than I – only confirmed this. His words – that there would times in life where I'd give it all up for a cuddle – echoed within me. And I had to admit to myself that, in all honesty, his words rang true. Already, I was beginning to sense that, in the years to come, the longing for a partner, for an intimate relationship or for having my own family would at times lead me to question my certainties and my commitment and vows.

Back then in my most honest – or perhaps insecure – moments – I reflected in subjective mode, full of romantic ideals, that no life could possibly be lonelier than that of a celibate. That was why the promise of future battles, or the longing for intimacy, was both a challenge and a blast of truth. Would the Jesuit life offer another way to channel our feelings, banish our loneliness and embrace the lives of others? Would we manage to be a different kind of family? Would our future entail loving everything and everyone, as Bishop Casaldáliga had indicated in his impressive 'forewarning to some young men aspiring to be celibate', or would we turn into crabby, taciturn bachelors, morose about paths unchosen? Many demons haunted me then.

Yet now, quite a few years later, I can say with confidence, after having helped many couples, that the perception I had then that 'no life is more lonely than that of a celibate' was complete nonsense. In fact, the life I've chosen has led to my heart and mind being full of people I'm very fond of, lovely memories, affection, shared experiences and warmth, even if at times I've also yearned for the choices I didn't make. Over the years, what I have discovered through talking to people about their private lives is that loneliness exists – as does the possibility of truly encountering others – in every life. What is true is that every life is different. I've often recalled in sorrow those prophetic words about how the longing for a cuddle would make me question my convictions. Today I sense that sometimes it's far lonelier to share a bed with your lifelong partner when you are separated by a wall of silence, a problem or a deep-seated interior wound, than it is to sleep alone. Why? Because loneliness, that untimely lover, has many guises.

Part One

3

The Signs of Loneliness

The word loneliness covers a variety of very different experiences. Each of us would probably define loneliness in a different way depending on our individual stories. So, before we begin to reflect in depth on the reasons for loneliness and its potential solutions, it might be useful to look at some of the signs of loneliness. This will allow us to make a closer inspection of all its manifestations. We can safely state that the experience of loneliness is varied (like a travelling companion with many guises) and that it's subjective (because we don't all experience it the same way, even though we may be in similar situations, which is why there's no one-size-fits-all solution). In some ways loneliness is a real paradox: you can feel alone in the middle of a crowd, yet you can feel accompanied in the middle of a desert. Finally, we can safely say that sometimes loneliness is welcome and sometimes it's painful.

A Travelling Companion with Many Guises

There are many instances in literature of travellers who appear to pilgrims in various guises. I like to use this image to describe loneliness. It's akin to a travelling companion whom we sometimes encounter by chance. Yet it has many faces and names or, to put it more prosaically, there are different types of loneliness. Without trying to make an all-encompassing generalisation or implying that we all experience loneliness in exactly the same way, let's think about how, for instance, we cope with loneliness in its various guises at differing ages.

Psychologists say that even infants experience loneliness. This is linked to parents being either absent or distant, a phenomenon regrettably common today when adults are often outside the home due to heavy work schedules, last-minute work emergencies and excessive working hours. Meanwhile, children are often kept hyper busy to mitigate the absence of their parents. This phenomenon is connected, above all in the West, with the lack of other children to play with in homes where very often there is only one child. It's not easy for very small children to process the changes involved in the family break-ups so common today, nor to adapt to living in two homes, and having to relate to their parents' new partners and sometimes to the children of the partners' previous marriages. In such set-ups, children have to adapt to different weekly routines according to whom they are living with. All too often the help children receive is professionalised and delivered by school psychotherapists or psychologists. They are doubtless necessary, but are simply no replacement for the security offered by a stable home life and children spending plenty of time with their parents. I imagine that for some children loneliness means a vague longing and sense of absence, and a demand for affection. For others, it may take the form of an indefinable sense of discomfort, arising from spending more time being stimulated by electronic devices than through interacting with other children or adults.

What of teenagers? They also have to cope with times of loneliness: for teenagers, the world seems simultaneously both small and too big. Teenagers feel too grown up to be treated like children, yet are still too young to be treated like young adults, even if they already see themselves as adults. They have to go through a time of great change, which adults don't understand. At home, their parents are no longer an infallible source of authority and instead become the one authority a teenager will question more than any other. That's supposing that we're not dealing, as is sometimes the case, with those children who behave from their earliest years like mini-tyrants with their elders. As a teenager, you feel misunderstood by adults, but, at the same time, there are certain things you'll never tell them because they're just the type of things you think will push adults away. Why? Teenagers feel under pressure to show that they're confident and strong, decisive and successful. The pressure to shine is huge – even more so today when young people are active from such an early age on social media, where the sole aim is gaining likes and followers. The compulsion to show off and attract others makes the need to shine all the more desperate. Reality, however, comes in shades of grey, and teenagers know this. However cocky they might seem, they're aware of their insecurities: that they may not be as good-looking, athletic or successful as others seem to be. That's a best-case scenario. We're not talking here about teenagers who feel rejected, unwanted or unpopular, or those who have to scrabble for recognition or acceptance from the inevitable leaders who, at this critical age, have the power to decide who belongs to the group and who doesn't. If a teenager is openly rejected, or is the victim of any degree of bullying, whether it's in the form of a snide joke or full-on intimidation, who can they really speak to? All too often adults appear to overlook the issue, so to tell them what's going on would in a way confirm a teenager's feeling of being a failure, or reveal a want of courage or a fragility that's hard to admit at any age, but doubly so at a time when fitting in with the group seems to be the be-all and end-all of life.

That's one of the tragedies of adolescence: the group sets the trend at an age when developmental maturity is inconsistent. Furthermore, teenagers have to cope with their own growing pains: the quest to find their own identity, the conflicts associated with first love and the contradiction between a body that begins to resemble an adult's and a mind still struggling to grasp the complexity of relationships. That's why for teenagers so much is dramatic and extreme. Their emotional range is more prone to be black and white than shades of grey.

The young adult will also experience loneliness. Some of this will be identical to that experienced during a prolonged adolescence, including loneliness induced by personal complexes, rejection, the need to be liked, the fear of not living up to what you perceive to be others' expectations etc. We idealise young people, but actually being young today means being under constant scrutiny. And that's not easy. At this stage of life, many challenges need to be overcome to ensure that young people don't get trapped in a prolonged adolescence. At the same time, other situations crop up that are replete with new and frightening challenges that no one else can save us from. Perhaps this is most noticeable with the decisions you have to take on your own. In childhood, adults look after you. When you're a child, they carry you everywhere. Physically, a small child needs to be watched over constantly, protected and held in place, like a toddler who needs to be strapped into a car. When you're a child, adults decide how you spend your time, where you go on holiday, which school you go to, what you do at the weekend and your choice of extra-curricular activities. Likewise, adults decide if you'll go to catechesis classes or whether you'll be brought up without religion. And, although as a teenager you start to fight your own battles, you do so with a safety net: the knowledge that, at the end of the day, if you make a mistake, your parents will take responsibility for you.

A time will come when that's no longer the case. There are some vital decisions that only you can take because they will determine your future. No matter whether your choices turn out to be spot on or a disaster, you alone will have to deal with the consequences. Decisions including what to study at university, where to work, when to start a serious relationship, and whether to leave the parental home and become independent will become increasingly important after you come of age and until you are about thirty. Other decisions might include whether or not to prolong university studies as a last-ditch attempt to postpone entering the adult world, or whether to accept a first job. Do you have the courage to commit to a relationship? Are you ready to have a child? All these decisions, or others like them, become pressing around this age. It's a bit scary to realise that whatever you do, it's down to you to decide and then deal with the consequences, whether positive or negative.

Becoming an adult, and realising that this means finally growing up is also a bit frightening. There's that feeling of disbelief the first time a younger person addresses you as 'Sir' or 'Madam', or 'Mr' or 'Mrs'. If you're an adult you'll know what I mean. If you're not, you'll soon find out. You may take being addressed formally like this almost as an insult and snap back, 'Call me by my first name.' We've all been there and thought growing older just wasn't going to happen to us. That's why we so often hear that getting older is no big thing and entire generations try to convince themselves of the truth of banal phrases such as 'forty is the new twenty-five' or 'Age is all in the mind. You're as old as you feel.'

Part One

Rubbish. Being forty means being forty: four whole decades old. At forty, you're no longer a teenager.

Yet growing older is hard. The mid-life crisis, which for some people happens before they hit forty and for others a bit later, creeps up on all of us at some point. It's the moment when you finally realise that time is marching on, and that already you've lived half a lifespan. You think about where you were twenty years ago and where you'll be in twenty years' time and you don't even want to think about it. You need to process the fact that you've now left behind a carefree existence, and your commitments, which you once embraced with such fervour, are now tinged by routine and even, when you reflect on all that's now firmly behind you, occasional melancholy. It's a time to evaluate your successes and failures. Perhaps the lacunae outweigh the successes. Perhaps your professional achievements have not been all you hoped for. Perhaps you've passed the halfway mark in the long-distance race of life in a position somewhat worse than you once imagined. Perhaps your children are no longer at an age where they're easy to handle and their rebelliousness or indifference hurts you now more than you'd like to admit; deep down you have terrible doubts about whether they love you as much as you love them. Perhaps your relationship has settled into routine and habit and, sometimes, yearning for the passion and carefree days of yesteryear, you ask yourself what you've done wrong, without realising that what you are experiencing now is also love. Just another kind.

Then you ask yourself if it's all been worthwhile. You have to admit that some of your dreams have remained just that: desires that never materialised due to a lack of opportunity, a want of courage or simply bad luck. Yet this doesn't mean that you're not happy. Neither does it mean that you've failed or that you want to give up on the life you do have. Neither is feeling this way a betrayal of your spouse, your children or your vocation. It's just the discovery that the passing of time is solitary. No one else can live this for you. And the day of that discovery comes as a jolt. Then you finally admit that you've got older: a fact that can't be argued with! It's also relative, as to other people you may be still be a spring chicken. The perspective of time is like that.

Finally, we reach old age, which also knows loneliness, in particular three main types. The first concerns health. Ageing is hard. You begin to experience the aches, pains and failing strength you once witnessed from a distance in others. The carrying of heavy items, going upstairs and walking fast, things you once did without stopping to think twice, now start to require constant effort. And you're reluctant to admit that you're struggling. It irritates you that you need to visit the doctor more often. Sometimes you even try to hide your failing strength and symptoms, refusing to appear too vulnerable.

The second type of loneliness is inactivity. Of course, growing older doesn't necessarily mean being forced to sit in a chair to watch the world go by. There's a huge, indeed ever-increasing range of activities on offer for those in their so-called 'third age', an age category which, as health care improves, is ever expanding. Even so, many older people find that they feel lost and don't really know what to do once they're no longer busy with whatever previously filled their days. This change may be accompanied by a feeling of being unnecessary, or useless. The fear of being de trop, of being a bother, really gets to some people and they have to fight not to feel cast aside.

The third type of loneliness concerns death. It comes in two ways. The first, a gradual, sharpening realisation of one's mortality, a phenomenon that once appeared distant and to do with others. Questions about the meaning of life, its finite state, and life beyond death become more pressing. On the other hand, you find you are saying goodbye to friends of your own generation. Relatives, friends and acquaintances who were all part of a past teeming with life and good memories begin to die. The gap they leave is not easily filled.

If, instead of referring to different age groups, we speak of other dimensions of life, it is soon apparent that loneliness is manifest under equally diverse guises. I said earlier that the loneliness of a celibate was not the same as that of a married person. That's true. Being on your own means you don't have a partner with whom to share intimacy and tenderness. Being alone may also mean having a partner yet feeling distant from them, perhaps due to poor communication, problems or difficulties or simply the weariness that creeps into some relationships. Being alone can mean not having children by a certain age. It can also mean having children and not knowing how to get through to them; or accepting their distance at certain times when you see them being friends with everyone except you, but not allowing this to make you give up or feel discouraged. Quite different is the loneliness your children experience when they feel simultaneously rebellious and guilty because they don't know how to respond to parental nostalgia for a time they have long since left behind.

The loneliness of unrequited love is not the same as the loneliness of never finding that special person who makes you feel the centre of the universe.

Many who are coping with long-term illness and who sometimes feel misunderstood, ill-accompanied, or treated with condescension because of the limitations imposed by their condition also experience loneliness.

Some vocations are by their nature more solitary, such as that of the intellectual who spends long hours among books, dedicating time, energy and talent to delving into a particular area of knowledge about which they may only be able to talk to three or four fellow experts in the world.

This kind of loneliness, inherent to specific vocations, was magnificently summarised by the novelist Paul Auster. During an interview in which he looked back over his life, Auster admitted: 'Sometimes I wonder why I have spent my life shut away in a room writing when the world outside is full of life and possibility. Writing demands that you give yourself to it completely, opening yourself up to every conceivable type of pain, joy, to every conceivable emotion. To write well requires moral courage. No other occupation asks the person who does it to surrender their whole being, mind, heart and soul without knowing whether in the end there will be any reward.'[4]

Then there is the loneliness of the leader who knows every aspect of occupying positions of power and responsibility. There is also the

---

4. *El País*, 1 September 2017.

loneliness of the long-distance runner, to quote the title of Alan Sillitoe's story about rebellion, self-improvement and achievement.

Other types of loneliness are linked to art, hobbies or faith. What is certain, as the title of this chapter suggests, is that loneliness is a travelling companion that appears at different times in our lives and in varying guises.

Is There a Cure for Loneliness?

I should just add an amendment to what was said in the previous section to clarify that however much we might generalise and flag up widespread traits of loneliness that crop up more frequently at particular periods in life, not everyone – even if sharing such traits – will experience loneliness in the same way. Neither will every single child, teenager, young person, adult, old person, celibate or spouse or anyone else match the descriptions given above.

Our experiences are closely connected to our own personal story, our upbringing, the values instilled in us in childhood, and with any traumatic incidents (whether minor or major) we have survived, as well as our past relationships and our character, which is shaped partially by all this and partially by our genes and biological make-up.

To put this another way, loneliness is a subjective experience. It is worth being clear about this, otherwise it is easy to fall into offering solutions to others and forgetting that what works for one person is not necessarily right for another. Advice based on our own experience, such as 'I'd advise you to do … ', needs to be complemented by time spent listening to another person and trying to understand what they really mean when they say anxiously, 'I feel alone'. This is because feeling alone doesn't necessarily mean feeling unloved. Sometimes it may do. At other times, it is really about feeling a failure, or reaching one's limits, or tiredness, or even competitiveness or guilt or insecurity … The list of what those words might mean stretches ad infinitum.

That doesn't mean that we can't share our experience or give advice: it wouldn't have been possible for me to write parts of this book if loneliness were a phenomenon so subjective that we could never put ourselves in another's shoes. However, it does mean that there is great scope for nuance, and, for that very reason, for learning from others.

Loneliness in a Crowd and Encounters in the Desert

A third characteristic of loneliness is its paradoxical nature. At first sight, we might think that being alone concerns a lack of human interaction or the absence of close ties to others. According to this, anyone who is surrounded by and constantly interacting with others will never feel lonely. Whoever lives in silence far away from their loved ones will feel the pain of their absence. However, that's not really true. Not always, anyway.

Is it possible to feel alone in a crowd? Yes. You can feel alone even when your life is full of people and socialising, even when you don't have a moment for yourself and you are surrounded by people who ready to advise or help you. It may even be the case that when you are really busy, the lack of quiet time on your own is the main barrier to your really being present to others.

When you feel like this, others may feel like a burden, a demanding, even slightly invasive presence. An ever-present family, an all-consuming group of friends, a possessive partner, or any relationship based on dependence may be like this. While they don't leave you with any time for yourself, they somehow manage to leave you feeling isolated.

At the other extreme, the desert may also prove a place of encounter. By desert, I mean those wide open spaces where the silence is tangible and your significant others are, for whatever reason, at some distance. However, such an experience, when lived out in peace and without feeling pressure, may be something you choose, which, far from isolating you, helps you to deepen your connection with others. Some people, for various reasons, seek a little quiet, silence, tranquillity and distance from others. Others withdraw in order to find themselves – and be available to others. Others still will discern on a solitary urban walk more real human interactions than they perceive in a room alive with chatter.

Introverts need their own space, time and rhythm of life, but this doesn't lead them to living in isolation. Finally, there are those with whom you have such a solid, settled and free friendship that, even if they're far away, you feel they are part of your life, both now and in future.

Loneliness as Friend and Foe

We often load the phrase 'being alone' with connotations of pain or failure. Yet being on your own it is not always disquieting or painful. Even though we often picture loneliness as scary and anxiety inducing, an experience to avoid at all costs, there is a kind of loneliness that is both desired, sought after and fruitful. Who hasn't said at some point how amazing it would be to have their own space? If you have the time, resources and kind of work that allows for this you may sometimes withdraw, and feel good in your own space and company. Some people, by nature, are just more solitary. They enjoy being alone, apart from others, and having time to themselves, and fill their time with activities that don't involve relationships.

Examples of this kind of nurturing solitude abound: an afternoon spent just in the company of a good book that allows you to plunge into the lives of others and travel with your imagination to exotic destinations you leave behind on the last page; a time of prayer where the Word of God or the search for this in-dwells in your solitude; a long meander through a city, where you imagine the lives of those who cross your path but also rejoice in their distance. You undertake such journeys alone but in a spirit of being open to meeting others. It's easy to dance with this kind of aloneness, perhaps because its heart song is easy and less shrill to the ear.

However, another type of aloneness is painful, even warranting the word 'vicious'. It's unsought, unwanted and unacceptable. This is the loneliness we truly fear, which rears its head whenever someone says, 'I feel alone', in anger, in pain or because they're missing someone. It might also be an abstract statement, echoing a vague desire for a future filled with others, as yet unknown but whose existence you sense. This is true for singletons, saddened that so far they haven't found a partner with whom to share their lives, intimacy and dreams. Perhaps they don't yet know the name of their missing other half, but they feel none the less the emptiness caused by their absence.

There is also a more specific kind of loneliness, where, rather than missing an abstract unknown 'other', you mourn the absence of a particular person: for example a loved one whose death has left with you with a void that nothing will fill. Or perhaps you're missing someone who was once a key part of your life, and who now, for whatever reason, is distant, and you're in a period of separation. It might be due to a past romantic relationship, when with painful nostalgia, you remember times shared together, episodes now irretrievably anchored in the past. Or perhaps your loneliness concerns an unrequited love, which still gets to you, punishing you with questions, with blame and fruitless desire. Or perhaps it is because those you trust are out of reach, a situation perhaps fuelled by your insecurities, anxiety or fear of rejection.

It is far harder to handle this kind of vicious loneliness. This is a dance whose song is shrill, loud, or else unheard, a deafening silence. It leaves you desperate to wail, to strike out, fight back, to twist the hand of fate and scream to the heavens the names of those who are keeping their distance. Why? In situations like this, we experience loneliness as a failure, as being abandoned or rejected or as a sign of our own limitations. All that is much harder to process.

In this book I want to address this vicious type of loneliness, this torturous tango which, despite our faltering steps, we must learn from. I want to suggest an alternative and viable heart song for this tortured dance, one that will help set our spirit free.

Part Two

Reasons for Loneliness

Do people today feel lonelier than in the past? Are we experiencing separation, isolation and absence more than previously? A fellow Jesuit, who had spent quite a time outside Spain, observed with surprise and concern, after returning for several weeks to see his family, that one of the changes in Spain that had struck him the most was that the spread of social media and the increasing use of electronic devices, far from leading to a more close-knit society, was instead generating greater social isolation. He concluded his observations with an interesting question: 'I wonder if the Church should try to offer a spirituality of loneliness for this world where so many feel alone?'

Social commentators often concur that loneliness is increasingly widespread in the West. Conferences, debates and reports are devoted to trying to figure out the reasons for this. Sociological studies, meanwhile, are accumulating a wealth of data about the rising number of urban single-person households in every age bracket. Already, some comments on this phenomenon have become clichés, for example the paradox of such isolation in our hyper-connected society.

The question is whether loneliness is more prevalent today than in the past. Has it always been part of the human condition? What contemporary factors or experiences most influence loneliness or make it particularly acute and painful?

In the following pages I will aim to outline a few reasons for modern loneliness, on the understanding that, as with every generalisation, my efforts will prove on the one hand inadequate, and on the other, excessive. However, my aim is to help the reader to respond, and perhaps see themselves in some of the examples given, as well as reflecting on other types of loneliness that I don't mention.

Part Two

First, a forewarning. Part Two is demanding. It's not a feast for the senses because, being an outline of the reasons why loneliness can hurt, this material may highlight some very challenging and very human dynamics which are likely to stir up painful memories. I know that if I were writing about reasons for joy, for example barbecues with friends, our heart songs, the books that set our imagination free, a lovely lightness of being, the beauty of creation or the positive energy of modern-day society, the outcome would be joyful. But sometimes we need to enter dark storm clouds in order to reach the light shining on the other side.

What I do promise is that Part Three of this book will be open to hope. Just as I'm now about to describe how loneliness may attack or paralyse us, in Part Three I'll aim to introduce some joyful concepts and describe the steps that may safely guide us through facing the darkness.

In the following chapters, I will explore three separate reasons for loneliness. The first reason is intensely connected with our personal stories, the second with the information-heavy society we live in, and the third encompasses the major psychological wounds of people today.

4

A Few Personal Reasons

I use the phrase 'a few personal reasons' as shorthand for the aspects of modern life with which we all have to struggle alone. These intimate experiences begin within ourselves, and sometimes we have to face them alone. I'm going to focus on five specific aspects that are particularly widespread in our everyday lives.

Living Alone

The first is the most obvious. Many people feel alone because they are. For decades, the number of people who live alone has been on the increase in many countries. The Continuous Household Survey from Spain's National Statistics Institute in 2016, for instance, showed that in Spain 25 per cent of all households were single-occupancy. This trend appears to be increasing in each consecutive report.[5]

Among those who live alone, a large proportion are over sixty-five. However, living alone occurs in every adult age range. Perhaps it's due to increased life expectancy, which leads to more people outliving their spouse or partner, or with instability in romantic partnerships or marriages, or the number of childless couples or households. It may be linked to the increase in people moving to a different region or country. This makes it harder to put down roots and obliges families to live far apart, leaving some members more isolated. All this has an impact. The consequence is that single- or dual-occupancy households are now more common than larger groups of people living under one roof.

5. Instituto Nacional de Estadística, http://bit.ly/2pn9Xc9.

For many people, being alone for hours in an empty house surrounded by four walls and silence, even if it's relieved by the television, radio or their computers, is overwhelming and painful. They feel they have no one to call or talk to. The occasional news report about an invalid who died weeks, months or even years before they are missed, shocks us into imagining their daily lives: the long, empty hours and the absence of routines shared with others. Who hasn't occasionally seen an old person about to pay in the supermarket and trying to stretch a brief moment of chit-chat into a conversation, as others look on in irritation, without realising that this short interchange may be the only conversation the pensioner might have that day?

I don't mean that everyone who lives alone finds it problematic or indeed the source of an unfulfilled emotional need. Many choose to live alone, while others have plenty of friends, contacts or social groups outside their home. Yet the reality and the facts show that increasing numbers of people are living alone, not out of choice but because they have been left on their own.

There's No One Like Me – Losing a Shared Identity

Zygmunt Bauman's concept of the 'liquid society' is still an apt description of the world we live in. When the great Polish sociologist defined the modern world as being 'liquid' what he meant was that many of the solid structures that once held our society in place are now diffuse and fluid. Which is why all we have now is a 'liquid life', unstructured and uncontainable, ebbing and flowing in all directions.[6]

Many aspects of our lives have become fluid (or liquid): religion, politics, culture, moral values, how we conduct our relationships and our fears. Perhaps one of the most fluid and fascinating examples of this loss of mutual reference points involves our personal stories. They too have lost their solid structures, firm outlines and predictability to become

---

6. Zygmunt Bauman, *Liquid Modernity*, Cambridge: Polity Press, 2000.

narratives so unique, individualised and complex that we find it hard to identify with each other's lives.

So what do I mean when I say that our life stories are no longer solid or that they or are 'becoming fluid'? Decades ago, people of the same generation would have a relatively stable and fairly similar outlook on life. Social conventions and predictable and unchanging life patterns made it easy to place the phase of life somebody was in. For example, someone who had married and worked in a certain city was highly likely to reach retirement in the same place in the same company and to bring up their children in a stable household that would withstand the passage of time and the ups and downs of communal living. Social mobility was neither sudden nor frequent. People found it quite easy to relate to their social peers, and groups of friends lived through fairly similar and normal life situations.

That doesn't mean that everyone's lives were identical, because people in the past were just as unique as they are now. What it does mean is that once we all had a very similar lifestyle, and being familiar with this helped people feel secure when they looked at their peers. The counterpoint to such stability was probably that lifestyle patterns were fairly rigid. As with almost everything, this familiarity had both advantages and disadvantages.

In contrast today, our lives are far less predictable because the world is changing at a dizzying pace. It is said, for instance, that the main jobs of the year 2030 have not been invented yet; how can people possibly prepare for this?

Being able to work anywhere, whether in your own country or the world at large, has become a must for younger generations, who are constantly on the lookout for career opportunities or the chance for personal fulfilment anywhere on the planet.

Modern education does not offer much in the way of stability either. Educational systems are multiplying, as are the educational pathways within them. As a result, when we meet someone a few years our junior, we often can't relate to them at first, because we can't assume that they have gone through the same educational stages that we have.

Types of family group are also multiplying and diversifying at such a fast pace that one can no longer predict what kind of relationships the people we know might have. Today, a teacher of a class of ten-year-old children has to be careful to avoid making generalisations about the type of family they come from. Why? It's highly likely that a large percentage of the children are living in family set-ups which, only a few decades ago, were practically non-existent: parents in second relationships, children living with half-siblings, or joint custody arrangements which mean they live part-time with each parent.

All this leads, somewhat inevitably, to us being unable to relate to one another. It's not easy to identify with people whose lives you can't begin to imagine. It's hard to know what they've been through, the decisions that have led them to where they are now, let alone the personal, professional and emotional journeys they have endured. None of this is easy to work out, nor can you assume that they will understand your own life and insecurities.

Very often loneliness is due to a lack of community and roots. Anyone who has to start their life afresh in a new place confronts the arduous task of meeting and then getting to know new people, acquaintances who later become friends. If, on top of this, we factor in our lack of time and the frantic, accelerated pace of life, it is easy to understand why people have increasingly few opportunities for a profound encounter with others. Yet we have a plethora of social media platforms designed to help us to find like-minded people. Users describe themselves and the traits they either have or would like to have, in the hope that this digital space may yield a kindred spirit or, indeed, their other half.

It's really not easy to identify with the lives of others. This is one of the principal challenges for post-modern people, who, in their overwhelming insecurities and fragmented state, long to find a healthy way to be individual without being sucked into the crowd.

I Wash My Hands – The Temptation of Innocence

It was the French philosopher Pascal Bruckner who coined the expression 'the temptation of innocence'.[7] It describes a relentless trend in contemporary society: the habit of washing our hands (and conscience) by claiming we are not responsible for anything. Bruckner links this watering down of our sense of responsibility to our ability to make ourselves always victims, regardless of whether we are genuine victims or actually perpetrators. He also connects this to our habit of declaring our innocence at all times and in all places.

Bruckner's analysis is twenty years old, but time has not proved him wrong. All too often, whenever responsibility has to be taken for something we don't like, we get tangled in a web of accusation, disparagement and blame. Politics offers a perfect example of this type of dynamic. The guilty are always somewhere else, whether the scandal involves corruption, a bad decision or a crisis of any nature. The fault always lies with the system, with other people, with the international situation, or with individuals who have no ties to any particular political party. Any argument is valid is long as it gets us off the hook so that we don't have to put our hands up and say, 'It is our fault.'

In order to acquire a sense of responsibility, we need to be taught it. However, teachers all over the world often complain today that they feel abandoned by our society and by parents. Once it was normal for parents and teachers to be united in their demands of pupils. Unfortunately, today it is all too common for parents and their children to form a united front in discrediting teachers. A dominant spirit of overprotection in our society decrees that we should not demand too much from children or they will end up traumatised, or worse still, rebel against an adult authority which is injured the more it is questioned.

The consequence is that children are not taught to take responsibility for their own behaviour. Instead, the focus is on living in the present moment and avoiding the consequences of their actions. The opportunities for doing that just multiply. Obviously, this is not an absolute rule.

---

7. Pascal Bruckner, *La tentation de l'innocence* [essai], Paris: Grasset, 1995.

There are people, schools and initiatives that teach children responsibility by preparing them for a future riddled with dilemmas and critical decisions. However, more often than not, the time for young people to make commitments and bear the consequences is delayed. I'll give an example to illustrate this.

You may have encountered a scenario similar to this in a church school. A pupil is reprimanded or sanctioned for some kind of inappropriate behaviour. The teacher responsible for imposing the punishment is besieged by the child's parents, who come to the school to intercede for their child. A prolonged negotiation ensues to see if the punishment can be avoided. At one point, the parents will almost certainly attempt to 'demonstrate' that the pupil was right, and the school authorities, wrong. All kinds of personal arguments will be aired – the teacher has it in for the pupil, the real problem is poor teaching etc. If this approach proves unfruitful, or if the bad behaviour involved can't be disproved, another line of argument is deployed, along the lines of, 'But … he's only a boy.' This line is used whether the student concerned is twelve years old or a university student living away from home. Then, suddenly, the parents attempt to minimise the seriousness of the child's behaviour, in order to prove that either their child is fragile or else simply unaware of their behaviour. And if that doesn't work either it is common – above all in Catholic schools – to hear the parents' final desperate argument: 'But you're priests. Shouldn't you be forgiving?'

So where is the pitfall in such scenarios? What is the real problem? Essentially, the issue is that education should not be about over-protecting children. True education consists of helping children to face the facts and understand that every action has a consequence, whether positive or negative. They need to learn how to process and deal with such consequences, even when these prove upsetting or uncomfortable. We really are not helping young people by shielding them from reality because in the adult world they won't enjoy that protection. It's far better to learn integrity in minor matters in order to show integrity later on with major issues.

What this vanishing sense of responsibility and evasion of difficulties produces are adults who are utterly clueless about how to face failure or their own mistakes. Both are inevitable at some point in life. We all find it easier to share our successes and triumphs than our failures and mistakes. If no one has ever prepared you to confront the difficult parts of life, then failure will prove far more disturbing. If you've always had someone to point the finger at when things in your life go wrong, to use as an excuse or to blame for the consequences of your mistakes, you'll feel very alone the moment they are no longer there and you can't avoid your own responsibility any longer. Yet many people seem unable to process failure as just part of life. Instead of moving forward afterwards, they get stuck in a cycle of self-pity and blame, and go round in circles licking their wounds.

All That Glitters Is Not Gold: Why Does Everything Go Better for Everyone Else?

Another source of major anxiety today is the apparently wonderful lives led by others. It can feel like everything is going swimmingly for everyone else. In our society, with its focus on superficial appearance, it's easy to assume that everything you lack or yearn for is completely sorted in the lives of the people you know. You regard them from a distance with yearning, longing, even envy.

Perhaps the reason for this is that we lack the time to get to know each other properly. (Further on in this book I'll address the challenges of learning the art of conversation.) This time poverty leads us to base our opinions about the lives of others more on appearances than on hearing the truth from the horse's mouth. All too often appearances are deceptive because we conceal things, hide what embarrasses us, or act out of pride. None of us likes to reveal our shadow side, emotional torment or the inconsistencies in our behaviour that make us look weak, or the battles we have fought and lost.

Perhaps the problem lies with us being overexposed in both the real and the digital world to the seemingly ever-present happiness of others. The French philosopher and sociologist Gilles Lipovetsky, who has been analysing the contemporary world for decades, summed this up when he said: 'We are everywhere bombarded by pictures of escape and promises of pleasure. The walls of our cities are covered with billboards showing signs of perfect happiness and liberated eroticism. Snapshots of holidays radiate a blissful happiness. What with advertising, the multitude of ways to spend your spare time, activities, games and fashion, our day-to-day life is saturated with praise for entertainment, the pleasures of the body and the senses, and easy living. With this cult of well-being, fun, happiness here and now, the ideal of an easy, hedonistic, playful life is in the ascendant.'[8] The problem is that the life we have to deal with every day is also serious and monotonous and routine. Yet, as that is a truth we are exposed to less and less frequently, it can easily seem as though all everyone else does is party.

This impression may be reinforced by the overload of information we receive via self-created social media profiles. We see this for instance with platforms like Facebook or Instagram, which feature highly contrasting posts: news, jokes, criticism and, of course, tragedy. However, usually this is a media tragedy: an item of international news concerning faraway wars, earthquakes or hurricanes in regions you've heard of but which seem to be in another galaxy; or news of lives devastated for various reasons; or stories about victims who, at the end of the day, almost always seem to be a long way away. In fact, when an unexpected tragedy strikes lives similar to our own and in close geographical proximity, the impact is massive because it's such a shock.

However, when it comes to our personal connections on social media, what we tend to see most, above all with close contacts, is the lovely side of life. Think of the pictures that people put up on social media: they almost always show happy, beautiful people, brilliant smiles; groups of friends or several generations of one family sharing magical moments; people on their own, blissful and at peace while on holiday, or just relaxing, or having a good time. We read enthusiastic posts about people's achievements which they share and celebrate with gratitude. We may also read the comments from their friends telling the world how much they love the person concerned, how much they mean to each other or

---

8. Gilles Lipovetsky, *De la légèreté: vers une civilisation du léger*, Paris: Bernard Grasset, 2015.

how much they value being part of their lives. We are silent and slightly anonymous spectators of these highly intimate declarations, whose authors express powerful, deep feelings of affection for those they love. Children suggest their mother is the best in the world. Fathers take pride in being their children's most trusted confidant. School friends are still friends despite living in different countries, or the passage of time.

Sometimes, almost without realising it, you get the impression that everyone else has the most fabulous life. That's because the less fabulous side of life, including our emotional wounds and relationship problems, aren't on show so much. What we don't reveal on social media – and surely we are right not to do so on this open window to the world – are our sleepless nights, our difficulties, our breakdowns, the relationships that might be torture for us, the projects stuck in limbo that will, in all probability, turn out to be failures. We don't expose our fears, insecurities or ugliness. When we put up a photo that we like, we don't also post the other twenty of the same moment in which we have come out a little worse, or appear less glamorous or festive, and where you can see clearly our wrinkles, beer-gut, our age or tiredness. All that we get rid of and wipe out. And of course we never photograph all those times in our lives that are monotonous or anodyne. The Cuban poet José Martí once wrote: 'You should love the time of effort / you should love the hour that never shines / if not, you should not say that you've tapped the truth.' The hour that never shines is that of our everyday routines. And learning to love it doesn't just mean tolerating this because there's nothing else we can do. Neither does it mean that our routine or greyest hours are a burden we have to take on, or a parenthesis amid times of entertainment, brilliance or fulfilment. It is rather that so much of our lives and relationships are lived and built during those grey hours that we need to learn how to value this time.

Imagine a world where everything one sees of others is lovely and deserving of celebration. If you don't fully realise that this is an incomplete picture, you may start to think that other people have much better lives than yours, that your lot in life is only greyness, failure and self-sacrifice. A priest may view family life through rose-tinted spectacles. He may indulge in dreams of a warm hearth and home, where the intimacy of a spouse awaits the husband and together they celebrate the accomplishments of their children. However, that same father of the family whose life the priest fantasises over might remark, sometimes in jest, at others times seriously, how well priests live. He in turn may envy what he perceives as the priest's independence, time to himself and lack of financial worries. What is missing from both scenarios is an awareness of the very real difficulties in each case. This could include the difficulties of communicating within the family, the tension between love and loneliness in that of the celibate; or the demands, in the father's case, of a schedule that has to adapt every day to the needs of the family. Or the hardship for the priest of living with the constant scrutiny of an anti-clerical society. Every life has its battles, but by not showing them, sometimes we end up hiding them, and hiding them to excess, to the point where we end up believing there are no battles at all.

This illustrates the saying that the grass always looks greener elsewhere. However, let's be clear. This isn't a crude or straightforward dynamic. It's not as though we spend our lives envying what others have, or licking our wounds or feeling sorry for ourselves because of what's missing in our own lives. We are probably all more or less aware that each of us has our own battles and struggles, our good days and bad nights. It's just that it's one thing to know this, quite another to really understand this in our hearts through sustained contact with others. This is because all too often we engage only with what we see of others while they engage only with what we let them see of ourselves. That's why another's sparkle tends to dazzle us when we feel overwhelmed by our own shadows.

Partial Communication – The Loneliness of Casual Relationships

A few years ago, a film called *Crazy, Stupid, Love* became popular. An interesting, pleasant comedy, it concerned personal relationships and various ways of experiencing love, all framed within several generations of the same family. One of the characters, Jacob Palmer, is a young, charming businessman who takes pride in avoiding relationships. He flits from one amorous conquest to another without remembering any of the women involved. At least, that's until he meets Hannah, an unconventional young woman, who begins to surprise him by her independence. She doesn't seem too impressed by his Don Juan tricks and postmodern yuppie airs. One night when, at last, she appears to be interested in him, he invites her to his home for a drink, fully intent on yet another night of forgettable passion. However, as the hours tick by, Jacob begins to feel something new. He realises this girl is not like the others. She laughs at his seduction techniques. He really enjoys being with her. He doesn't want to treat her like the others or for her to become just another notch on the bedpost. As they start to exchange trivial confidences – who is buying on the telly-shopping channel or what brands of clothing they like to wear – Jacob begins to let his guard down. At the end of this evening of cosy chatting, Jacob offers Hannah an unusual invitation: 'Ask me a personal question,' he says. Pausing for a moment, she replies, 'Tell me about your mother.' Deeply moved, he starts to open up: memories, longings and ancient wounds eventually pour out of him. That night Jacob sleeps in Hannah's arms, but they don't have sex.[9]

Jacob's request – 'Ask me a personal question' – has become for me something of a shining light or beacon of maturity. We live in a world where relationships are built on many dynamics, except perhaps the very one that might help most with bridging the gap that separates us. We relate to each other out of self-interest, for professional reasons, for entertainment or leisure reasons, out of attraction, from desire, or need, or habit, but where is the place for the most personal, intimate dimension of a relationship? This dimension of a relationship, which for some people was once irreplaceable, has now become much harder work. If it happens, it's at the end of the road, not during the first stages of a relationship. Today, for example, many people opt to completely disconnect sex from personal intimacy. It becomes just a pleasurable

---

9. S. Carell and D. Di Novi (producers) and G. Ficarra and J. Requia (directors), *Crazy, Stupid, Love*, Carousel Productions, 2011, https://bit.ly/2TnvqDB

physical exchange, something impersonal that is not intended to bond you to the other person. If love comes, it will be much later, and trust, communication and personal questions lie a long way ahead in the future.

Likewise, many social networks today allow users to establish all kinds of links without ever meeting in real life. It often seems as though no one has the time or feels the need really to get to know the other. It's as though the easiest option is to enjoy the advantages of closeness but without any corresponding requirement to deal with its demands.

The skill of communicating associated with relationships has now fragmented. Just like a modern supermarket, which offers the consumer an infinite variety of similar products, each subtly different from the next, we too are offered the chance to select our romantic experiences. Want 'Love with no relationship?' 'Head for the centre aisle.' 'Anonymous sex?' 'Next to the low-fat margarine.' 'Monosyllabic one-night stands?' 'In the special offers section.' 'People who share your interests but won't hassle you later?' 'That'll be in the leisure and free time zone, just next to the eco-friendly make up.' 'Permanent relationships?' 'I'm sorry, we no longer stock those.'

Sometimes, all of the above happens to us without us even realising. It's not as though this is a conscious decision, as if you choose to give up communicating or trust or saying no to a profound encounter with another person. In fact, it's quite possible you might well long for this, and really want to find it. It's just that actually doing so is becoming so challenging, and on the way you find so many alternative offers, that the temptation to make do with a substitute is ever greater.

The problem is that this kind of disconnected sex, a physical exchange with no emotional encounter, does not relieve people of their loneliness. The writer Mario Vargas Llosa nailed it when he said, '"Light" sex is sex without love or imagination, purely instinctual, animal sex. It meets a biological need but it does not enrich the life of the senses and emotions and it does not bring couples closer together beyond the sexual coupling. Instead of men or women being freed from solitude, once the peremptory and fleeting act of physical love has passed, they return to solitude with a feeling of failure and frustration.'[10]

Here, however, is some good news. People still long for communion and connection. The longing for something that goes a little further, for a lived-in intimacy, a closeness that encompasses true friendship, love or feelings of belonging has not disappeared. We still think it worth making an effort for a lasting relationship. Even when someone seems to give up or to make do with what I've termed 'partial communication', they still do so with a yearning for finding a connection that goes beyond a fleeting sexual encounter. The hope that a 'significant other' might exist and be found is easy to see when we take the time to reflect a little, perhaps because we are, in essence, made for connection and communion.

Probably the most complex aspect of this is finding the quality time with which to build solid relationships. Such time allows us to grow close, to get to know each other, to sound out each others' characters, and to open up to each other gradually. One of the hardest things to learn nowadays is the art of deep conversation. That brings us to the second tranche of reasons for loneliness, those pertaining to our social media-driven world, where the very forms of communication that promise to bring us ever closer together run the risk of isolating us even more.

---

10. M. Vargas Llosa, *Notes on the Death of Culture: Essays on Spectacle and Society,* London: Faber & Faber, 2015, p. 497.

5

Is the Media to Blame? Communication Lockdown

Before I begin to explore a few traits of our society connected to the proliferation of social media platforms and technology – which I'm neither attacking nor demonising – I'd like to clarify that I don't see them as the source of problems or difficulties. Neither do I wish the reader to conclude after reading what follows that things were better in the past, or that people communicated with each other more then, or that the past was a golden world of authentic relationships.

What I do believe is that the world of information offers us tools. These tools in themselves are neither a curse nor a blessing but rather an opportunity. What we do need is to learn how to use them and also to detect the tricky dynamics into which they may lure us. As my theme in this section is loneliness and the lack of communication in contemporary society, my analysis will highlight problem areas, but I would like to emphasise once more that today we can no longer imagine a world without the Internet, just as we don't yearn for the world before the invention of fire, or the printing press, or electricity or the arrival of cars.

We'll now look at the dynamics which, in our hyper-connected world, may contribute to making people feeling even more alone.

Why Do We Never Talk Like We Used to?

This might sound like something a nostalgic couple might say as, after many years together, they regard each other with unease and lament the loss of their once fluid conversations, yearning for the happy-go-lucky, carefree chatter of their youth. Actually I'm not really going to talk about this kind of nostalgia for the past in relationships, although it does happen. I want instead to focus on a more social dynamic: the loss of our ability to converse. It is fair to say that it is becoming increasingly difficult to have conversations. This, in part, is because we no longer have the time to spend with other people, but also because we need to learn the art of conversation.

While social media networks and digital communication are relatively recent phenomena, it's worth remembering that other forms of mass communication are also relatively recent. After all, the first television programmes are barely eighty years old. It is hard for us now to conceive of silent households devoid of any kind of virtual or digital connections to the outside world. Yet, until only a short while ago, that silence was a reality for most of the day the world over. People talked more, because they had the time to and they wouldn't or couldn't fill that time with other things. Perhaps they spent more time reading and in silence, but it's highly likely that they also spent more time talking.

Conversation is an art that requires an apprenticeship. I don't believe it is something so neutral that it can be learned just by following a few rules. True conversation depends on many factors, including character, context and culture. Some nationalities are more reserved and others more talkative. Some people are more reserved, and others more loquacious. Some people can talk until they are blue in the face, others turn a monosyllable into an art form. The content of conversation may vary greatly, from the banal to the sublime, the trivial to the memorable. It may be impersonal or intimate. That is all true. But, having said that, we have to ask if we have too little time for deep and tranquil conversations, those chats during which we gradually lower our guard, and daily chit-chat gives way to familiarity. This leads to the sharing of confidences. This cannot be improvised, nor can it happen as soon you meet someone new. Intimacy takes time. At times, it even requires boredom, familiarity or routines that lead to shared activities. It is akin to a gradual manoeuvre for drawing closer in which two (or more) people get to know each other. They size each other up, investigate each other and come closer, until at last they let down their guard, and each is able to see who the other truly is.

Perhaps I am idealising conversation a little, but isn't this a bit true? The theory that I advance here is that although such deep conversations exist they are rare, more so than in the past, and that is due to the increase in mass methods of communication in our daily lives. There are several reasons for this.

On the one hand, this is due to the omnipresence of social media, which prevents us from feeling alone or having a need to somehow fill the silence. Today, people don't feel the need to talk whenever they are in a queue because their mobile phones provide them with occupation and entertainment. Who hasn't seen dozens of rail passengers – and perhaps you were one – on a platform, all furiously tapping away at the screen of their mobile phone while waiting for a train? Conversation is not even essential at home: all too often people eat with the television on, and live at a fast pace, while those who share a home may live quite separate lives.

On the other hand, the media and digital platforms provide us with endless topics of conversation. That might seem to contradict what I've just said, but we tend to talk about whatever subjects we have to hand. Of course, there's always plenty to talk about. The question is whether the things we chat about help to fill our deepest longing for affection and contact. We bond with others on the basis of the latest trending news topics. Thus we spend hours commenting on Trump, missiles in Korea, the latest political scandal, the latest bomb attack devastating a city, or else the match of the day or the latest controversial soundbite from a public figure. We do find time to talk about these things, repeating our opinions. We echo what we've heard on chat shows, read in newspaper columns or voiced on social media. Sometimes we even formulate our own opinion, but this almost never comes into those personal conversations that strengthen our bonds with each other, expose our vulnerability or build bridges between us. It is, however, these more personal conversations concerning our dreams and our dark places, our fears and our desires, faith and doubt that enter this muddy terrain of solitude, aloneness and encounter.

Let's add in another factor. Today we talk more often from a distance than face to face. WhatsApp chats in particular have invaded our daily lives. They have their own rhythms: interactions are limited to a mix of immediacy, abbreviations and brevity. No variety of emoji, however many we invent, will reproduce the nuances of the emotion we convey in conversation. When we speak to each other face to face – or when we write letters to each other – we may use a countless variety of words to express joy, fear, sadness, revenge, pain, shame, embarrassment, shyness, boredom or any other mood we're in. What's more, when we speak face to face, not only do we communicate through our words, but also through our hand gestures, the expression in our eyes, our blushes and speed of breathing. Even the bags under our eyes and our smiles are expressive. Yet, all too often today we have to make do during mobile phone chats with emojis: a smiling or crying face, a frowning icon, a thumbs up or a danger sign. We are thus losing our linguistic ability, subtlety and nuances. We are also losing the spontaneity and the emotion produced by face-to-face conversation. In WhatsApp groups users sometimes openly blame others for things, but when they meet up in person, they are not able to say what is really going on. Increasingly we live in world where people say 'I love you' far less in person and send far more 'I love U' messages across a cyberspace devoid of passion or human presence.

Communication as a Minefield

Another widespread trend today is polarisation as an accepted form of behaviour. Everything seems to be about taking or aligning with different sides, or extremes in speech and behaviour. The world is divided into those who think like us, and those who don't. There's no middle ground. Those who take extreme positions flag up new ways of discrediting anyone who refuses to enter into battle. So anyone who doesn't want to annihilate someone else verbally is accused of being lukewarm, distant, a 'goodie-goodie', a demagogue, or of not wanting to get their feet wet. Anything goes to cancel out the arguments of those you disagree with, to justify your own orthodoxy and never question your own convictions. This happens in politics, sport and social commentary, and, of course, religion. Everything is susceptible to becoming a source of trench warfare.

Many people understand the word dialogue to mean debate. By debate, they mean combat, akin to a tournament in which rivals must confront and destroy each other, until only one is left standing. There's no desire to have a reasoned argument or explore nuances, and far less to listen to the reasons of your opponent. There's zero desire to understand each other, and, of course, no one ever wants, in such debates, to change in any way at all. Instead, the aim is to crush your opponent, reinforce your own convictions and where possible to discredit, while you're at it, anyone who thinks differently. Insults, cruel jokes and sarcastic nicknames are the order of the day.

So why does this produce loneliness? Because this dynamic, which has taken over public debate and is now spreading relentlessly, isolates anyone who refuses to get involved in a confrontation.

In my first book, *En Tierra de Nadie*[11] (In No Man's Land), I described how I perceived the Church as a triangle. In the first angle were militant Catholics with a rigid faith, in the second were activist Catholics with a politicised faith, while the third angle was home to every brand of anticlerical Catholic. I attempted to describe the unequivocal and clear-cut positions of each group, who used their corner of the triangle to draw together everyone who thought as they did, discrediting everyone else. Later on, however, I ventured to speak for all those who found themselves somewhere towards the centre of the triangle, in no man's land. These were the people who didn't have everything cut and dried: with some aspects of Catholicism they felt more attached to tradition, in others they leaned towards a need for change, yet on other points they felt more distant from the Church. They were not choosing an à la carte Catholicism, but being faithful to their formation and conscience, nor could they, nor would they, want to identify with either group at the extremes.

My experience over the years is that there are many no man's lands. Not only in the Church, but also in politics, in culture and in how we perceive the problems afflicting our world. No man's land is, in fact, the

---

11. J. M. Rodríguez Oliazola, *En Tierra de Nadie*, Santander: Sal Terrae, 2006.

middle terrain occupied by many. I'd actually go further: it is the terrain of the silent majority. And many people in this no man's land believe they are alone because they are not hearing opinions with which they identify in their own insecurities, confused feelings or nuanced opinions.

So why do we not hear these more cautious, nuanced and complex opinions? It's because the world hands the megaphone over to the extremists who shout the loudest. Social media, with its two golden rules of making an impact and brief communications, works by demanding that users make dramatic, controversial statements. Those who make the biggest noise are not prone to be subtle and considerate but rather to be provocative, and they know just how to grab the headlines with a hurtful accusation or melodramatic remark. Furthermore, digital platforms allow people to feel they are anonymous and may act with impunity. Sometimes the anonymity is real, and people are hiding behind generic identities, false profiles or fantasy avatars. Even without the excuse of anonymity, a strange thoughtlessness prevails that makes people who in real life would be reasonable and adopt more nuanced positions to lose all common sense and restraint. They make comments on the Internet which are far more outrageous than anything they would say in real life.

Our digital platforms, in short, are colonised by barbarians, who push and shove, love and hate each other, know and persecute each other. There aren't many of them but they're very vocal. And the vast majority of social media users – who are silent and polite – feel alone because they don't realise that the most vocal and the most defensive are just a partisan, histrionic minority. The silent majority fails to realise that the world is not as hostile and merciless as this cyberspace full of self-appointed judges who assume the authority to dispense at will verdicts of condemnation or approval.

5,000 Friends

Once upon a time, with a hint of hopeful naivety, the Brazilian singer Roberto Carlos sang, 'I want to have a million friends'. The idea of a million was by any measure over the top, an impossible if rather graphic exaggeration. Because no one can have a million friends. Or can they?

That was before Mark Zuckerberg began Facebook to allow complete strangers living far away from each other to connect online and share their tastes, lives, photographs and stories. In order to limit Facebook connections ad infinitum, the network decided that individual users could have a maximum of 5,000 friends – although no such limit applies to the official Facebook pages of celebrities. Not bad, if a bit far off Carlos's ideal figure. But who wouldn't be satisfied with such a huge number of friends? You would definitely be described as popular!

Yet the truth is that the concept of 'friends', when applied to social media platforms, is, at the very least, over the top, if not downright deceptive. This is another petty contemporary niggle: many people, lacking contacts in the real world, take refuge in social networks where they make far more tenuous, volatile and superficial connections, which are both fuelled by and restricted to the network itself. These are connections that begin and end with one click on the keyboard. In fact, they are effectively long-distance relationships, restricted to whatever you want to reveal about yourself on the social network and limited to the interests you share with others.

Of course, all kinds of virtual relationships are possible. Many people today actually begin what prove to be enriching and deep relationships via digital platforms. However, it's also true that social networks often allow us to mask our interior emptiness, conceal our inner silence and distract us from feeling alone.

A few years ago, the following story was published in the Spanish press. José Ángel, a man from Vigo, a city in the north of Spain, died in radical solitude. He lived surrounded by rubbish, and suffered from Diogenes syndrome (a disorder that includes a compulsion to hoard) which had led him to isolate himself from family members, neighbours and acquaintances. For more than a week no one missed him or realised he was dead. Unfortunately, this is a phenomenon that occurs far too frequently, so much so that it is no longer news the way it once would have been. What made José Ángel's case special and brought the news of his death to the media was the discovery that, in contrast to the limited, isolated life he led in his city, he was active and popular on Facebook, where, at the time of his death, he had no fewer than 3,544 friends and 361 followers. On Facebook, he revealed little about his own life but published opinions and posted news on current affairs. He expressed concern about the environment. He took a stance on matters to do with the countryside, current affairs and life in general. What was surprising was the contrast between his virtual life and his real life, between his many virtual friends and his actual loneliness. A few days after his death, a woman from Tenerife, with whom he communicated frequently on Facebook, was concerned by his persistent silence, so she contacted the police. His body was found shortly afterwards. Thus the only person to miss José Ángel was a woman who lived 1,677 kilometres by sea (1,042 miles) from Vigo. She alone among his 3,544 Facebook friends noted his absence sufficiently to worry and take steps to try and find him. This shows the limit of this virtual world, and how it can become a refuge for the lonely.

Zygmunt Bauman put his finger on this when, speaking of the fragility of human connection, he observed: 'It seems that the most seminal accomplishment of virtual proximity is the separation between communication and relationship [...] "Being connected" is less costly than "being engaged" but also considerably less productive in terms of bond building and bond maintenance.'[12]

Chasing 'Likes'

Black Mirror is one of the most disturbing television series of recent times. It is a commentary on technology and its possibilities or, to be more accurate, its dangers. The series isn't set up as a friendly, futuristic form of sci-fi but a dystopia, i.e. snapshots of a terrible world too similar to our own simply to dismiss with a shrug of the shoulders. Each episode tells a separate story which takes to an exaggerated extreme an existing major or minor aspect of the world of modern communication: the volatility of public opinion, the existence of ever more sophisticated

12. Bauman, op. cit., p. 1170.

and minuscule devices that may end up able to record everything we do, digital blackmail, and every facet of life being turned into televised entertainment.

The first episode of the third series is titled 'Nosedive'. Its plot is unfortunately all too familiar. Society is ruled by how popular people are on social media. According to their social media ranking, people are either included or excluded from various situations. The main character is desperate to be liked, and this determines all her behaviour.

As a starting point, although it is taken to extremes, this episode is not so far-fetched, given the dynamics that prevail today in digital contexts, including the desire for followers, and the pressure to obtain 'likes' for your posts, photos or any other content you post online. And the episode also shows the downside of all this: the hordes of haters, as those who turn social media into something more akin to a boxing ring than a space for exchange or dialogue, are known. All this is the order of the day. Many people feel under pressure to be liked online and act out of panic that they may be rejected.

Let's take three examples. In June 2017 the singer Ed Sheeran, one of the most successful singers in recent times, announced that he was leaving Twitter because he could not process the number of negative comments left on his feed by complete strangers, who apparently hated him. 'One comment ruins your day,' he confessed in an interview. It was a noteworthy confession from someone who, in 2017, became the most-streamed artist on Spotify. He was the most listened-to singer in the world, and No. 1 in forty-one countries. However, he just could not cope with online harassment. The love-hate dynamic at work on social media is too much for many users, even those who are more or less accepted.

At the other extreme is the story of Australian model Essena O'Neill, who became famous thanks to her photographs on Instagram. Her followers – in their hundreds of thousands – had led to O'Neill securing well-paid advertising deals. In November 2015, she also announced she was leaving social media platforms. In her case this wasn't because she had suffered rejection but was due to her being overly popular and accepted. She was spending too much time doing everything she could to be 'liked': preparing her photographs, scrutinising every picture and getting obsessed about beating her own Instagram records. When she decided to abandon social media platforms, O'Neill explained that she had realised that the Instagram world wasn't real life but a digital fantasy in which everything is aimed at gaining approval. The price – she said – was her own life and self-esteem.

On 20 September 2017, Celia Fuentes, a well-known influencer, committed suicide. Why would someone so popular, so young, and with an apparently perfect life kill herself? The initial surprise when the news broke soon gave way to reports revealing the true nature of her social media presence: she had created the fantasy of an ideal life but her real life was lonely and dogged by failure. She felt under pressure to be 'liked' and to increase her virtual attractiveness. The downside was insecurity and feeling she had to reject anything that might be imperfect. 'It's all a lie' was the last message Fuentes wrote on WhatsApp.

There are countless other stories like these. I'm not trying to make a general rule on the basis of the examples above, but there is no doubt that, as already mentioned, this constant tension between praise and rejection, approval and insults, followers and indifference conceals a dynamic in which attaining 'likes' becomes a must. Having endlessly to seek approval, even from complete strangers, is a fail-safe mechanism for creating feelings of extreme loneliness.

This pressure to be liked is extremely dangerous, and not because we are all keen to be 'influencers'. The problem is that it can also become an obsession in the most ordinary, everyday activities. The need for constant and reinforced approval can end up enslaving us. Why? Well, at the end of the day, obtaining a 'like' or followers for a photo or comment we post on social media is not what this is about. It is as though each 'like' is actually evaluating who you are. It's easy to blur boundaries and end up thinking that you, not the post or the photo, are what is being 'liked' or rejected.

In the episode of *Black Mirror* mentioned above, it's only when the main character, fed up and exhausted, finally gives up on fulfilling social media expectations, that she manages for the first time in ages to have a personal conversation with a man in the same situation. And she is able to laugh.

6

Existential Reasons for Loneliness: Three Great Contemporary Wounds

Spanish poet Miguel Hernández defined the three wounds that we all will suffer at some stage: the wound of life, the wound of love and the wound of death. Life buffets us. Love unsettles us. Death stuns us when we see others die and remains an enigma until we too meet death. To paraphrase Hernández, I would like to propose, varying his words only slightly, the three great wounds of the modern world, which have led us to the edge of doubt and disquiet: the wounds of love, of death and of faith.

The Wound of Love – Stripping the Daisy

Think of someone pulling petals off a daisy as they sigh, asking if their love is requited. It's a vivid illustration of many people's anxiety and insecurity about love today. The proof lies in the reams of books and articles published on the topic. The reason? It's increasingly rare for us to share common ground on which to build a relationship. We can't agree once and for all on what we understand love to be. That makes togetherness hard work. Fewer couples are finding that they share a solid emotional base on which to build a life together. Who today can say a relationship is 'for ever'? Worse still, who today can trust that 'for ever' doesn't really mean 'for as long as this relationship lasts', or 'for as long as this suits me'?

Some time ago one of the most widely read newspapers in Spain published an article on relationships with a provocative headline: 'Fifty years sharing your bed with the same person. Seriously?'[13] The article explored how the concept of what a couple is and what the family is has changed. Today, it explained, the idea of love lasting 'until we stop enjoying ourselves' carries greater weight than being '[together] until death', and because of this people look at love through a more pragmatic, perhaps more sceptical lens. The article begins by emphasising how volatile love is:

> In the last few decades the phrase 'until death do us part' has gone from being a romantic desire to a kind of life sentence capable of discouraging the most loved-up boyfriend or girlfriend. While 20 or 30 years of marriage was once the norm, with the increase in life expectancy (80.1 years for men and 85.6 for women, according to the National Spanish Statistics Office) a marriage could now last 50 years. In fact, marriages in Spain last an average of 16 years; a statistic which reveals how few couples celebrate their silver wedding (let alone golden wedding) as most of our parents did. And, as we usually marry in our 30s (33.2 years old being the average age to marry in Spain, according to the National Spanish Statistics Office) before we reach our 80s we'll still have the chance to enjoy two or three more marriages.

So why do I speak of 'the wound of love?' Is this deliberately choosing to see the glass as half empty? Shouldn't we see the flexibility described in the article as something liberating, freeing people from rigidity and inertia?

The pitfall of the cycle of nuptial enjoyment described here is that it involves only a short-term marital relationship, which neither adapts nor matures, replacing the traditional relationship, which evolves and changes, flourishing in times of joy and maturing in periods of difficulty. Short-term relationships might be easier to handle, but they are also probably more volatile too. Obviously, we're not talking here about a casual superficial decision, akin to changing your jeans or phone, but

---

13. *El País*, 12 March 2017, bit.ly/390cPCN

rather how to build a solid relationship which may become the refuge and bedrock of your entire life.

In 2016, Krysti Wilkinson, a young American blogger, wrote an article about her generation, which was widely distributed and reproduced in the media across the world. It bore the headline, 'We Are the Generation That Doesn't Want Relationships'. It is a portrait – a little over the top – of a generation that wants the image of a relationship but not the effort of cultivating one. I quote below a few paragraphs that perfectly summarise the author's argument as well as what we are calling 'the wound of love'.

> We want the façade of a relationship, but we don't want the work of a relationship. We want the hand-holding without the eye contact, the teasing without the serious conversations. We want the pretty promise without the actual commitment, the anniversaries to celebrate without the 365 days of work that leads up to them. We want the happily ever after, but we don't want to put the effort in the here and now. We want the deep connection, while keeping things shallow. We long for that world series kind of love, without being willing to go to bat.
>
> We want someone to hold our hand, but we don't want to put the power to hurt us in their hands. We want cheesy pick-up lines, but we don't want to be picked up … for that involves the possibility of being set down. We want to be swept off our feet, yet at the same time remaining safely, independently, standing on our own. We want to keep chasing the idea of love, but we don't want to actually *fall* into it.
>
> We don't want relationships – we want friends with benefits, Netflix and chill, nudes on Tinder. We want anything that will give us the illusion of a relationship, without being in an actual relationship. We want all the rewards and none of the risk, all of the payout and none of the cost. We want to connect – enough, but not too much. We want to commit – a little, but not a lot.

We take it slow: we see where it goes, we don't label things, we just hang out. We keep one foot out the door, we keep one eye open, and we keep people at arm's length – toying with their emotions but most of all toying with our own.

When things get too close to being real, we run. We hide. We leave. There's always more fish in the sea. There's always another chance at finding love. There's just such a little chance of keeping it these days.[14]

Uncertainty, unpredictability, relationships without sacrifice, commitments that are easily broken, polyamorous relationships – a phenomenon so many defend and support nowadays – all these may promise freedom. They also involve a corresponding fear of losing what you do have, a fear that torments many people who, although sure of their capacity to love, may feel more insecure about their capacity to be loved. Qualms, fears and complexes conspire against us, wound and torment us, leading us to question what on earth is worthwhile. Therefore, we regard the future as threatening and a source of despair.

Bauman says that the modern pace of change also applies to relationships: 'Perfectly usable, shipshape cars, or computers or mobile phones in quite decent working condition are consigned to the rubbish heap with little or no regret the moment their 'new and improved versions' appear in the shops and become the talk of the town. Any reason why relationships should be the exception to the rule?'[15]

Pascal Bruckner, another great thinker quoted earlier on the temptation of innocence, describes the wound of love in our contemporary world as an excess of sentiment, meaning that when feeling evaporates, nothing's left. 'We are living in a hyper-sentimental period and today couples die because they put themselves under the jurisdiction of a cruel and merciless god – Love. It is not only whims or selfishness that put an end to couples, but also the quest for a permanent passion as the cement

---

14. *Huffington Post*, 29 April 2016, https://bit.ly/2wQ3ajX.
15. Bauman, op. cit., p. 335.

that will hold them together. It is the mad intransigence of these lovers or spouses who reject any compromise: either fervor or flight, no half measures.'[16] Obviously the God of love the French philosopher describes is not the Christian God, but an idol of fire, trapped in the quagmire of a demanding, insatiable feeling.

The idea of the wounds experienced in relationships, especially with regard to couples, is interesting. In *Amoris Laetitia,* Pope Francis refers to some of these wounds.[17] Throughout the encyclical he speaks of the different wounds of love, including mistaking commitment for being tied down, the challenges of truly encountering each other (both to communicate and in silence), the culture of casual relationships, indecisiveness and emotional-sexual immaturity, couples lacking the time for dialogue and to listen to another, selfish paternity and maternity (or the refusal to be parents), having exaggerated expectations of a partner and feeling let down in relationships, egotistical love and, of course, to quote from the Synod of the Family, the fear of loneliness: 'one symptom of the great poverty of contemporary culture is loneliness, arising from the absence of God in a person's life and the fragility of relationships'.[18]

All the above are wounds produced by a vulnerable, fickle and ephemeral form of love which, in some cases, becomes a caricature of romanticism, another form of egotism seeking affirmation, or a substitute for the strong, rock-like love so wonderfully described by St Paul in the First Letter to the Corinthians.

The Wound of Death – We Don't Talk about That

It is something of a paradox that in the West death is becoming a subject that we try to deal with as if it were taboo, to be silenced and eliminated from view whenever possible. It is equally paradoxical that

---

16. Pascal Bruckner, *The Paradox of Love* (Tr. Steven Rendall), Princeton, NJ: Princeton University Press, 2012, p. 85.
17. Pope Francis, Post-synodal Apostolic Exhortation, *Amoris Laetitia*, Dublin: Veritas Publications, 2016.
18. Ibid.

although death is so often hidden, it's almost the only certainty all of us have in common. Our only unquestionable fact is our mortality, despite the occasional boast of a few random scientists that they are on the cusp of discovering a foolproof method for delaying death, or have found the recipe for eternal youth, or how to turn back the biological clock. What's more, we have absolutely no guarantee that we'll live another year, decade or, indeed, any fixed amount of time from now onwards.

We work on the expectation and understanding that, give or take exceptional circumstances, it's normal to die once you reach a certain age. We assume that medical advances will manage to halt many diseases in their tracks – and that consequently life expectancy will increase. None of that can disguise the finality of death, that moment which levels us all.

Yet for decades our society seems, for various reasons, to have forgotten all about death. One reason is the decrease in infant and child mortality. This has made the concept of death being omnipresent rather distant, so death is now associated far more with old age, and reaching the end of a long life.

The universalisation of healthcare and therefore of people dying in hospital has made death in the home a rarity. Now people invariably die in impersonal hospital wards, which their relatives, after absorbing the bitter pill of their death, will never need to visit again.

The transformation of funeral rites and farewells into services intensely commercialised by funeral parlours and undertakers has also removed grieving from the domestic sphere. Can you imagine anyone today keeping vigil with a corpse in the family sitting room? A concerned friend or relation would instantly alert them to their lack of common sense: ever afterwards that room would be tainted by painful memories.

Excessive and erroneous ideas about the need to protect very small children from death means that they are often kept away from the funerals of their relations and acquaintances, because it's assumed to be better for them to be elsewhere.

Finally, the language we use about death is also a cover-up. We turn death into 'a parting', 'a journey', or we use the euphemism 'passing', which fails to answer the question of where the deceased are 'passing' on to. Hence the wording of death notices that announce that, 'Today, X has left us' or 'X is no longer with us' etc. We all understand perfectly well what this means, yet somehow these expressions allow us some latitude to look elsewhere, anywhere, rather than stare death in the face.

So what's the problem? Isn't all this, at the end of the day, a perfectly reasonable defence mechanism to protect ourselves from pain? Isn't this, in a way, a totally valid option given that many world views that speak of a life beyond the grave are in freefall and so many people lack religious beliefs that would give them hope or a sense that death has meaning? The first danger of covering up any direct mention of death is that it leads us to lose our sense of perspective. However, if it is part of our philosophy that life ends, the way we look at the world becomes radically different.

I'd like to flag up a very interesting video that is available on the Internet: at Christmas 2015, a set of organisations carried out an experiment about our perceptions, priorities and values. They asked a group of young people from Madrid, one by one, about the presents they were planning to give that Christmas to someone very significant – it could be whoever they chose. In most cases they opted for their mums or dads. Their replies were cheerful, normal, and, to a lesser or greater degree, creative. Then the group was asked a far more sensitive question: 'And what would you buy this person if you knew this was going to be their last Christmas? 'What if you knew that this person was going to die?' Suddenly, everyone began to look tense, and struggled to find the right words. When, at last, they replied, their answers were considered, thoughtful and poignant. Although the exercise was not easy, it was worthwhile, because the prospect of death suddenly gave the present moment a new depth. The presents they chose in this new context were redolent with significance, meaning and tenderness.[19]

The sad thing is that we've made this attitude and approach to death something of a privilege that we give in to only when death is imminent, when illness strikes or when we know without doubt that our time on Earth is limited. At such times, the future may feel too bleak or painful for us to gain a clear perspective. How often, when we are facing the

---

19. http://bit.ly/2eHqCEh.

death of a loved one, do we discover that what we thought important only a days earlier is actually trivial!

Today we have lost this perspective, which teaches us to prioritise what is truly important and to relativise many things in this ever fleeting life of ours. Neither do we accept we have more than one life, which is why our choices and the path we take in life are so important. We have locked away in an unreachable place our awareness of being finite. Thus we deprive ourselves of the opportunity to look at life with fresh eyes, and an alternative type of wisdom.

So, what does this wound have to do with loneliness? There are two answers to that question. One the one hand, death is something so ordinary, and we are so unaware of it, that we don't take on board the fact that our loved ones will die, and that each day shared with them is a gift, but is also finite. Therefore, we don't spend as much quality time with each other as we could.

On the other hand, by hiding death away rather than accepting it as an everyday, familiar occurrence, by convincing ourselves, that, as the lesser of two evils, it must come, but only at the end of a long life, we make ourselves terribly vulnerable when death is unexpected. Death almost always seems premature, but sometimes more so than at others. An accident, a child who falls sick, the death of a father in the prime of life: such deaths seem to go against the grain of a normal life span, so much so that they are hard to process. If this happens to you, even those closest to you won't know really how best to help you or what to say, because everything seems out of kilter. Consequently, your time of mourning may be incredibly solitary. Even though we know death is inevitable, at such times we may feel that life has let us down.

Some time ago, prompted by a very unexpected and challenging death that left many of my friends deeply upset, I wrote about what I called 'the principle of uncertainty', observing the need for us to learn to weep about death.

> Sometimes we don't know what to say or do, we don't understand anything. There are just no words. And silence doesn't seem to help either. Sometimes unexpected situations erupt with a bang,

an unstoppable urgency, turning our all our assumptions upside down. Sometimes the questions are deafening. And they bring us to the very edge of our understanding, beyond which all we can do is hazard a guess.

It's at that point we're in danger of going crazy, losing our footing, or drowning in a sea of rage. The great temptation at this point is to make ourselves the centre of the universe. But the world carries on just the same as it was before: with its dollops of cheer and tragedy. With its challenges. With its deprivation and opportunities. This is when we need to give ourselves permission to weep, to accept that we have the right to break down a little, to ask for a hug that consoles, or else permission to withdraw to a safe distance. (We each have our different ways of surviving or dancing in a storm.)

But also, in all honesty, we have to accept that the uncertainty of life was always there. That the world was always weird. That each day matters, That love dances, delights, and becomes a habit, but is also lost, yearned for and needs to be let go. And that God hasn't tricked us, because we always knew that life was this mystery.

The Wound of Faith – The Mystery of a Silent God

A society of believers, where the majority of people share more or less the same religious denomination and world view, doubtless helps those who are living according to that faith. Why? Well, everything in that society is geared towards making life easier for the believer. For centuries that was the situation in the West. Non-believers were stigmatised and often persecuted. Atheism was a rarity, a scandal and a source of rejection. People believed, worshipped and prayed, prostrating themselves before pictures showing biblical scenes and filling churches with statues of the saints, the main witnesses of the Faith. Without doubt, this had its dark side: the dangers of a faith imposed on people and a refusal to accept the value – which is accepted without question today – of religious freedom. This situation certainly made it far easier for people to live out a faith shared by the majority of society, firmly rooted in its culture, tradition and customs.

Today things have certainly changed. The nineteenth-century 'Masters of Suspicion' (Feuerbach, Marx, Nietzsche or Freud) questioned faith from various perspectives, opening a gap for doubt, disbelief and explicit apostasy, or, as happened far more frequently, the silent apostasy of the great majority. The twentieth century saw the arrival of new movements which continued this trend. Far more than any political ideology, consumerism became a religion with no other God except wealth and no church except large shopping malls (including online ones nowadays). Secularisation, as studied in different contexts and with differing characteristics, is a reality in a large part of the world. The twenty-first century has seen the prophets of the new atheism (Sam Harris, Daniel C. Dennett, Richard Dawkins and Christopher Hitchens) swept along by slogans about how liberating it is not to believe in God. 'Probably God doesn't exist. Stop worrying about it and enjoy your life', was the slogan British journalist Ariane Sherine used to promote the 'new atheism' on buses. Her initiative received quite a good reception.

In Spain, we also need to factor in the polarisation which invariably accompanies any major issue. We should also take into account the social reaction of the past forty years to the role the Church had in shaping society during the previous forty, a phenomenon closely linked to the dictatorship of General Francisco Franco. But it's not just about this: Spain is now a far more hedonistic society, and factors including an ignorance of religion, anti-Catholic prejudices, the Church's own scandals and a superficial approach to analysing faith-based issues have all contributed to the growing numbers of Spaniards who are critical of religion. Meanwhile, practising Catholics have to live out their faith in an increasingly hostile society. This has ended up creating a social context where religious belief is identified with superstition, the past or magical thinking. Many Spaniards assume with tranquil conviction that faith and science are incompatible and don't waste a thought on the fact that others might view them as complementary.

A little while ago something strange happened to me. I had presided over a nuptial Mass and afterwards I was chatting to the guests before the wedding breakfast at the reception, when a woman came up to me with her husband. I don't if she forced him or whether he came willingly, but she said, half-jokingly, 'Father, say something to him. He didn't come to the Mass and is only coming to the wedding reception.' I was poker faced: it was a bit of an odd introduction given I didn't know him from Adam. But he, with utter self-confidence, said to me calmly as he shook my hand, and with an air of wanting to explain himself: 'Well, you see, the thing is, I'm more a man of science.' He was so serious, so convinced he was right and so natural. He didn't turn a hair. Perhaps he didn't even realise that implicit in the very way he had explained himself was the idea that I, as a person of religious belief, must be an enemy of science. Quite calmly he had called me ignorant to my face – or at least declared my beliefs incompatible with scientific thinking – in just one sentence. That is what we have to deal with.

Today we live in a context – at least in Spain – where, increasingly, the most commonly accepted form of intolerance is anti-Catholicism. Anyone on social media is able to blame the believer for all the evils in the world, or for anything deemed worthy of criticism in the Church. Freedom of expression should be closely guarded lest minorities or diversity groups are offended – something that I think is a good thing, as freedom of expression should never become an excuse for gratuitous insults. However, that same freedom of expression can become a justification for praising controversial, even sick works of art that mock the feelings of believers.

All this is, of course, circumstantial and it should not lead to believers feeling excessively victimised. However, we also have to face the problems in our faith and the perennial dilemmas it raises, particularly the problem of God's silence in the face of evil. That is where we do run into problems. We have to face the distance of a God who leaves us experiencing the most difficult kind of loneliness, because, for whatever reason, he does not make himself manifest. Why does God, if he exists, allow evil? That is the great question of the discipline known as theodicy. The answer many give is either that God doesn't exist, or if he does, he's bad.

Surely if he created us he should take charge of us? Why does he allow us a freedom that allows us to let each other down? Why, if God is close to us, does he not allow us to see him instantly? We try to answer this by alluding to freedom, to a more spiritual form of presence, to Revelation (where we can already find the answers to such questions), but sometimes we all have to dance with the absence of a distant God.

In the face of all these questions – both social and spiritual, encountered as a group or as individuals – the believer has to learn to sustain faith a little counterculturally. That eternal question of God's silence is a huge challenge for believers, who see non-believers appearing to live amazingly well without any need to refer to a religion or a deity.

Due to this, some believers behave in a defensive rather than contemplative mode, taking refuge in religious groups with solid, well-defined identities. But the majority – that silent group mentioned in the section on no man's land – carry on the fight to obtain a faith that is a gift but also involves a battle. In times of insecurity, exhaustion or boredom, the questions 'Where is God? Why doesn't he make things clearer? God, our God, have you too abandoned us?' may arise in the heart of the believer.

I don't think it is worse to belong to a questioning minority than to be part of a comfortable majority. Perhaps the first context entails less inertia and a greater personal involvement in faith. Perhaps it implies a more purified, mature faith because there is no doubt that any believer today has to face questions that they never needed to ask themselves in the past.

Whatever the truth, however much support we may obtain from the community or group with whom we may share our life of faith, there will always be scary moments that we can only deal with alone. In these situations, faith demands a leap into the dark that no one else can make for you. That's when we pray with a faltering faith that takes us back to the Mystery of God, repeating the words of the Gospel, 'I believe, help my unbelief.'

Part Three

Tango for One

That's enough digging into loneliness. I warned you in the introduction to Part Two that this run-through of reasons why we feel alone might be a bit challenging because it would explore the very human dynamics that these disquieting feelings of abandonment or absence generate in us.

I like to say that we are made in the image of the God of encounters. The truth is that the loneliness we experience is not empty. The Gospels contain many stories where the response to loneliness is an invitation to encounter God. These stories become a mirror of our own lives. The characters, the words they say, how they relate to each other through their deeds, and the decisions they take, all change their emotional landscape. It is as though a new heart song fills the empty silence of their lives, transforming silence into a symphony teeming with life and with people. This is the soul music that enables us to dance with loneliness. I like to imagine that when we move, we're really dancing to a song we can hear inside us. 'Everything I will say to you, I sing inside me,' sings the Spanish singer song-writer Rozalén in a beautiful love ballad.[20] What a lovely concept, that we sing in our soul the words we will later utter as a battle cry, a speech, in silence, as a lament or a declaration of love. To the rhythm of this deep, compelling internal melody, both our external circumstances and our perspective change.

This symbolic concept of a dance is often toyed with in films, whether they're musicals or simply films depicting a world where movement and music become the narrative method used to tell the characters' stories. I'd like to mention three particular film scenes which for me are simply

---

20. Rozalén: 'Antes de vert', in *Cuando el río suena*, Ismael Guijarro (producer), 2017.

Part Three

magical. Each features this kind of compelling heart song that transforms the outside world.

The first comes from the film *The Fisher King*. Parry is a strange, crazy, unpredictable vagabond who, we soon discover, is in love with Amanda, a shy, solitary woman who doesn't even know that he exists. For a few exciting days, Parry guides Jack, an ageing and troubled radio announcer, through New York, showing him how he sees the city. In a charming scene, he takes Jack to Central Station, urging him to wait until Amanda appears, as she does every day at the same time at the end of the vast station lobby. As soon as Parry sees his beloved Amanda he begins to follow her through the crowds, and at that moment the station is transformed into a huge dance floor. And with the beauty possible only through the magic of cinema, in a second, the enormous crowd of busy commuters, usually quite indifferent to each other, become – in Parry's imagination – a throng of mingling dancers, dancing together with joy. When Amanda vanishes onto the platform, the normal noise and bustle of everyday life returns.[21] What lasts ever after in the mind's eye is that moment of spontaneous beauty, music and exuberant happiness.

In *500 Days Together*, Tom, a young architect whose job is designing congratulations cards, is madly in love with Summer, the new girl in the office. He does everything he can to win her over. Just when he thinks it's a lost cause, the unexpected happens. She returns his love. After their first night together, we see how, the following morning, when Tom goes out, the city seems different to him. Tom is delighted to hear the sound of the song 'You make My Dreams'. He looks into a shop window, seeing himself as Harrison Ford playing Han Solo. He feels handsome, happy and successful, and the city dances with him. Passers-by smile at him and the park turns into one big party. Spellbound by the music of love, the entire city has learnt how to dance.[22]

Finally, *La La Land* is a proper musical film, so it's scarcely a surprise when the characters start to sing and dance. The magnificent scene at the

---

21. D. Hill and L. Obst (producers) and T. Gilliam (director), *The Fisher King*, Columbia Pictures,1991, http://bit.ly/2gnSLjP.
22. M. Novick (producer) and M. Webb (director), *500 Days of Summer*, Fox Searchlight Pictures (2009), https://bit.ly/2wwEFZa.

start of the film has now been shared, imitated, even parodied, to the point of satiety. Perhaps all of us would probably love to experience something like this. The scene begins with a long, sweeping shot of a traffic jam on the Los Angeles highway. Each car is a separate world: as the camera sweeps past each vehicle by we see the faces of the drivers, and hear voices relaying either their thoughts or else snatches of the radio programmes they are listening to. It's a glimpse into different lives and many different stories with little in common. Then the camera focuses on a woman sitting in her car. Her memories turn into a song. She gets out of the car. The song begins to spread, and the dancing begins as people sing 'Another Day of Sun'. The song weaves in one person's poignant memories, another's dreams, and the hopes, and pending choices of still others ... The highway fills with colour. Unexpectedly, we see a lorry become the stage for a band. The car horns become trumpets, and the car roofs become an improvised stage for the dancers as they celebrate another sunny day.[23]

The world is alive with joy and dancing, if we only know how to perceive this. Sometimes its mood is energetic, like an upbeat jig of victory. At other times, the atmosphere is more like that of a delicate, nostalgic ballet. Occasionally, the world's stage fills with a mingling crowd dancing in perfect harmony. At others, a soloist flits between shadows and the light, their steps echoing the shifting states of their soul. Dancing like this is a little like flying. It's a lovely way to navigate through life and relate to the world, to others, or to God. And yes, we can certainly dance with loneliness.

The Gospels don't say much – explicitly anyway – about loneliness. Sometimes we see Jesus praying alone. In the garden of Gethsemane that loneliness will prove especially stark and demanding. However, many Gospel stories allude to types of loneliness which, through an encounter with Jesus, transformed into a mutual heart song. In the next few chapters, I'll try to draw out some of those stories in order to interpret their heart song and the lessons they may have for us.

Let the dancing begin!

---

23. (F. Berger and J. Horowitz (producers) and D. Chazelle (director), *La La Land*, Black Label Media, 2016, http://bit.ly/2xClPf2.

Part Three

7

'Kid, Make Your Mind Up. You Can't Have It All.'

A few years ago, a fellow Jesuit titled his blog post with this snappy, arresting headline. The post was read with enthusiasm, sparking much interest on the digital platform where it was published. The headline made an impact because it suggested the exact opposite of what most people regard as ideal. In a world where having it all, doing everything, trying everything and never depriving oneself of anything is idealised, it was bold of him to state that you simply can't be everything in life.

In Chapter 3, in the list of personal reasons for contemporary loneliness, I mentioned how our lack of a sense of responsibility makes it difficult to make decisions. I said that we live in a world where a misguided sense of over-protection is depriving young people of the chance to learn how to make decisions, with all the consequences and responsibilities these may entail.

One fascinating aspect of the Gospels is their insistence that people need to make their own decisions. There are some things that no one else can decide for you. From the beginning, the story of Jesus involves people who have to take a stance and make a choice. There's an enormous arc from Mary's words, 'Let your will be done', at the Annunciation, until Jesus utters the same words in the garden of Gethsemane. In between those scenes, Jesus asks a huge number of people to make a choice. Jesus never demands, he calls. He doesn't impose his will, he suggests, he never compels people. He makes them an invitation. The people Jesus addresses always have an alternative option. The only thing they can't choose is everything. You can't have your cake and eat it.

To decide means choosing one of several options and then embracing your choice with enthusiasm. It also implies renouncing or leaving behind other options. Far from being a source of frustration or reason for sadness, the truth is that choice is a liberating heart song. Why? It implies that you have accepted that limitations are part of life, ignoring that treacherous whisper telling you everything is possible, so you are free to hear that delicate, subtle melody teaching you to accept and value what you do have – the gift of each day, your time and resources – because you know that these things are finite.

To decide involves taking a risk, even maybe making a mistake. Reading the story of the rich young man in the Gospels we feel that he made a mistake when he chose to return home and not to follow Jesus. At least he made a decision. Perhaps, further along his journey, his mistake will become a learning point and his previous 'no' will become a mature and accepting 'yes'. What is more problematic are those situations where people are not even aware they are making a decision. I've often reflected on the priest and the Levite in the parable of the Good Samaritan. Probably, in their decision to pass by the wounded Samaritan without tending him, there was something they didn't want to see, an unconscious decision involving a whole world of self-justification. If you are not aware of what you are deciding then you are likely not to discern the right decisions or grasp the impact of your mistakes.

None of us is exempt from making mistakes. Who hasn't put their foot in it at least once? It's not a big deal, even when you make a major mistake. Of course, it can cause upset, and if you do make a mistake you have to make amends where possible. However, the real problem lies in making a decision when you don't really know what you are doing. When that's the case, you really don't have a clue in which direction you're heading.

Think, for example, about the corruption that involves so many people and social institutions. Now imagine what would happen if a class of five-year-olds were asked about their dreams for the future. They might well say they dreamt of becoming footballers, models, pilots or doctors, or any other profession highly valued in society. Now, what if these children were asked if they wanted to be corrupt as adults (supposing we'd managed to explain to them successfully what this means)? Their facial expressions, probably something between a frown and a smile, would suggest that they didn't. Because corruption is bad, ugly and involves stealing. However, every corrupt person out there – unfortunately there are many – was once five years old. So when did they begin to slip down the path towards immorality, stealing public money or using their position for selfish, illicit ends? Their first decision to do wrong was probably small, almost inconsequential, and they had, perhaps, a justification. Perhaps they said to themselves it wasn't such a big deal, or that it made up for not being properly compensated in other areas of their work. The truth is that how we behave and the decisions we make in small matters will decide how we behave in relation to major ones.

So that's the background music. We're constantly, daily, taking decisions: How do I use my time? My words? My resources? What am I doing with the talents I've been given? Which paths do I choose? Or reject? How do I treat others? Furthermore, with whom do I choose to have dealings? All this, far from being a reason to be overwhelmed or discouraged is, if looked at positively, a call to greatness, to use freedom well, to cultivate a sense of responsibility and be aware of whatever opportunities are on the horizon.

It's just a fact that you have to take many of these decisions by yourself. Perhaps you might ask for advice, or for help with detangling complex issues when you reach a crossroads. You can also look for spiritual guidance, discernment and inspiration in God's Word and in God, who may be inspiring your questions. At a certain point in your journey only you can choose the path ahead. The wonderful part is learning how to decide, and gradually discovering where you want to go. This also means gaining clarity about where you don't want to end up at any cost. As I've said earlier, we don't have any guarantees we'll get things right. We can all make mistakes. Having said that, going crazy, taking risky, life-changing decisions on a whim or making decisions lacking any common sense is not remotely the same thing as being able to say lucidly and calmly: 'I know where I want to go.'

That is the game-changer: having a clear direction and a goal to aim for; drawing lines in the sand that are non-negotiable, and which you will not cross because to do so goes against your gut instinct; staking out key goals for the future which become your destiny. It is what you long for. These goals will direct your progress and pull you forward. Time and again, they will re-set your bearings.

This process of learning gradually how to make choices is one that will free you from unsettling doubts. With it, you will gain, little by little, an increase in confidence that will slowly diminish a paralysing sense of doubt. It also means that growing up isn't just a legal marker, but is really about embracing personal responsibility.

Part Three

8

The Tango of Expectation

Martha and Mary are the two sisters and friends of Jesus who represent well the tensions that are never lacking even in the best of families. The story narrated in the Gospel of St Luke tells how Martha, the older sister, fed up with doing all the housework and attending to the guests, explodes. She confronts Martha and even Jesus, who allows her younger sister to sit at his feet and do nothing to help.

Martha's outburst is one of the emotions with which we can identify most readily in the Gospels. She's tired. She's upset. The torrent of reproach she unleashes is probably the climax of a long period of pent-up anger, resentment and feeling abandoned. In fact, this episode is one of the few Gospel passages where someone explicitly mentions being alone. 'Don't you care that my sister is letting me do all the serving alone?' asks a wounded, furious Martha.

Most of the time our pent-up frustration doesn't end with an outburst. Instead, we cope with our feelings in silence, until perhaps they gradually settle down. However, there's no denying they exist. Sometimes, they exist in a wounded place inside us, leaving a trace of dissatisfaction or nostalgia for what might have been different.

There is a kind of loneliness that derives from dashed expectations, thwarted dreams or yearnings that never come to fruition. We see ourselves in Martha time and again, because we project our desires onto others. We lavish them with affection, and want them to respond to us the same way. We expect other people to act towards us in a certain way and when they don't, we feel low, sunk by misgiving, doubt and insecurity.

This is the loneliness of those who love more than they are loved back and, for that very reason, are always on the lookout for an unexpected caress, word of praise or tender gesture that they don't have to gain through effort or manipulation.

Volumes could be written about the loneliness of uneven romances because, while no two relationships are the same, all are somewhat unequal, and bear a burden of complexity and disappointment.

This type of loneliness is also familiar to those who wish to share with others their lives, time or day-to-day routines, but who sense that those closest to them are uninterested, caught up with other pressing matters, enmeshed by time pressure or other priorities. That's why there's never the time or the space for a meaningful chat, to exchange confidences or just to share a quiet moment together.

This is the loneliness of the person who, having a reason for celebration or joy, hopes others will rejoice with them to share or accompany their time of celebration in some way. Instead they meet a wall of polite silence. They are unsure whether this silence means indifference or blame, indicates a petty-spiritedness in the other person, or simply a lack of awareness.

The workplace is another arena that generates this kind of loneliness. This is what an employee feels when they hope for praise for their dedication, because they feel undervalued and unappreciated, but those words of recognition never come. Or it may be the loneliness of being somehow deeply frustrated by another's exhausting pattern of behaviour, but who never finds the right time or place to suggest a change. Instead, they brood in silence. It's the loneliness of the employee who feels they deserve a job that went to someone else. Or the person who, during a team project, feels they are putting in far more effort than anyone else, that others are failing to show equal commitment to the task at hand.

What all these examples share is that they involve patterns of expectation. We expect from others a kind gesture, praise or a particular type of conduct or behaviour. When none of this happens we have to process it alone. We can't always blame others for all this. Sometimes our expectations are at fault, and we're simply demanding from life or other people more than they can give.

At other times, perhaps we want others to guess what we feel, what we hope for and need from them. Yet we don't dare take the very simple step of just telling them, and talking through our frustrations. We keep quiet out of fear of showing our vulnerability, or because we are afraid of looking pathetic for asking for attention or affection. We keep quiet because we don't want to be seen as weak, or because we're acting out of a place of understandable distrust and think that if the other person isn't spontaneously affectionate, then how can we believe they're genuine if they only pay us attention after we've complained? All this is paralysing.

However, three changes of attitude bring fresh music to this tortured tango of expectation. The first is daring to open up to each other. When a relationship is meaningful, we need to have the courage to open up a bit to each other, perhaps not from a place of blame about what the other person isn't doing, nor by making demands – because whatever comes up should come from a place of freedom. Instead, we should be open with each other from a place of trust, revealing our insecurities, yearning and dreams. This opening up is our way of reaching out to the other person. Obviously, it's not always appropriate in every relationship to pour out our innermost feelings. But neither should hermeneutic silence be our usual pattern in relationships.

We are complicated. We make mistakes. We don't do the good that we want to do. Sometimes, without meaning to, we let others down. We need to understand that human relationships are everything apart from perfect. But they're also beautiful. And it is in relationships, in love, in friendship and through helping each other, that we share times of celebration and genuine communion.

Bearing all this in mind, the second change of attitude is to accept the gap between what one hopes for from a spouse or partner and what they're actually able to give us at a particular moment in time. We need to accept this, being aware that sometimes circumstances, or the upbringing or character of our other half may mean they are consumed by other personal battles or priorities, or simply that their character or way of expressing themselves (or not) is just different from our own. We need to accept this, not with resignation, but rather trusting that time can help us to adjust to each other's emotional rhythms and internal heart song.

The third change of attitude entails taking a good hard look at ourselves. Up until now we have focused on our expectations of others and how these may be disappointed. However, given that we all relate to each other from a place of expectation, we also need to acknowledge, in all honesty, the times when we haven't met the standards others expect of us. Perhaps this isn't really about changing our other half but rather about considering how our own words, affection, presence, silence, distance, tenderness or support may also be what others need from us. When we look at a relationship from this perspective, we may find that we need to cross a few bridges to reach our other half. And it may also be the case that sometimes, even when we know this, we are not able to give to others everything they expect from us. Yet that in itself is a lesson in accepting our own inadequacies, that sometimes we are not able to be equal partners in our relationships.

At the end of the day, we need to give ourselves permission to desire, dream of, long and hope for what others can bring us, without, however, turning a desire into a demand, a yearning into an obligation or a reply into a requirement.

9

What about Me?
Selfies or Snapshots

The Gospel of Matthew contains a fascinating parable about forgiveness. A man who owes a huge sum of money to his neighbour is unable to repay it and asks him to forgive his debt. The neighbour, feeling sorry for him, forgives it. That same man whose debt has been forgiven is owed a far smaller sum. When the man owing him the money asks him to pardon the debt, he refuses, insisting on being paid immediately, with the threat – which he carries out – of sending him to prison until he pays up. The parable ends with this selfish hypocrite receiving an exemplary punishment.

I don't think this is just a parable about forgiveness or selfishness. It's also about a kind of loneliness, which I call the solitude of the selfie. What's going on with the man who has been forgiven? He is relating to others only out of his own needs. He doesn't keep the bigger picture in mind or understand that other people also have their own problems and issues. What is driving him? When he meets other people all he thinks is, 'What about me?' Thus, when he sees his creditor, the only thing he is thinks, no doubt understandably, is 'I need him to forgive or at least delay the payment of my debt.' However, when he looks at the man who owes him a debt all he thinks is, 'I need him to pay me.' Under no circumstances does the big picture of what the other man might need or be going through enter his head. He doesn't wonder if the man he sends to prison has children, or if bankruptcy will finish him off, or if he has gone through a bad patch or whether, because his wife is ill, he can't work. For him, it would seem, other people don't matter, don't exist and are not his problem. To look only at ourselves is an exercise in convenience and selfishness. Sometimes we're not even aware we're doing this.

Something similar happens when we're only aware of our own problems, priorities, needs and timetables, or when relationships are built on the basis of whether they're useful to us rather than on the basis of gratuity and freedom, or when we place ourselves at the centre of the universe – whatever happens is only important in so far as it affects us.

Our personal and social interactions may reflect this 'selfie' mentality. Sometimes we notice that a colleague, friend or partner looks angry, or is silent or is keeping a distance, and we ask ourselves 'What have I done wrong?' We might feel uneasy, worried and upset. Yet most of the time when we ask, 'What's wrong?' the reply is, 'Nothing.' In fact, their anger, anxiety or distance has nothing to do with us, being about something else. The question we should perhaps be asking is probably about the state of their family, work or health, or whether something is upsetting or bothering them.

This is also true of our social interactions. For example, often our interest in the news is intensified when, due to its geographical proximity, it's likely to affect us. For instance, a terror attack in our local neighbourhood has infinitely more resonance than a terror attack in the streets of Baghdad, although in Baghdad, there may be an unusually high number of victims. Someone with Ebola in the streets of New York or London will generate more headlines than the thousands of Ebola victims in an African country we can barely locate on the map. Our 'selfie' instinct makes us automatically seek familiarity, a link to us. 'It could be me,' is the thought that stirs our anxiety and conscience. That's understandable, but this self-protective mentality, where we let in only what affects us personally, runs the risk of isolating us from the outside world. This is the loneliness of living in a world of selfies.

In contrast, life's rich colour is evident when we turn our focus – almost like adjusting a camera lens – outside ourselves towards others, without any expectation of identifying their lives with our own. No longer do we relate to them from a place of 'what I need,' or 'what can you tell me about myself?' Well-intentioned people sometimes say that we need to learn to see God in other people. Without denying this, I'd be satisfied if in our society we started by trying to see other people just as they are, if we learned to look at others beyond our own defences, self-absorption and immediate worries. The world of selfies is unstable and a little enclosed, but we can also live with our focus trained outwards towards the world, in order really to perceive and come to know others. This isn't like a virtual reality screen, keeping others at a distance and shutting down with the click of a button. It is a real commitment to seeing the essence of another. In doing so you let in real life rather than hiding from it; it's like photographing in all weathers, and exposing yourself to the cold, the rain, heat or wind. That outward focus is like opening a door through which you may go out to meet and to photograph the world.

There is a richness, beauty and a unique brilliance about human beings. We are all different, each of us is a mystery, a celebration, a separate world. Each of us brings a different heart song to the great score of life. Learning how to interpret and know another person is a journey full of surprises. To see another person is not about prying into their private lives out of unhealthy curiosity or an ill-conceived desire for gossip. It's about having a genuine interest in their story and wanting to understand those struggles that form part of every life. This is about seeing way beyond a social media profile or a few traits we may share in common. It's about being willing to get to know another person – and also to let oneself be known.

One of the most – if not *the* most – successful musicals of all time is *Les Misérables*. There are many reasons for its success. Victor Hugo's story of heroes and villains, love and forgiveness, guilt and redemption is moving. Yet the real reason it works is because the authors of the libretto and musical score achieved something rarely accomplished with such accuracy. Some songs are repeated several times throughout the show. Their themes are linked to particular characters or emotions (for example Jean Valjean, when he is about to take a momentous decision; or when Marius and Cosette sing of love; or when the Thénardiers, the fraudsters, return time and again to the same melody). There is a particularly impressive song at the end of the first act. The main character, Jean Valjean, starts to sing. However, here he's not singing one of the musical's many solos. Other characters take up the baton, beginning to sing one after the other. The adoring Marius and sensitive Cosette pledge eternal love, the energetic revolutionary, Enjolras, urges everyone to revolt against tyranny, the roguish Thénardiers get a slice of the action, the implacable Javert sings in defence of a law that he places above any other consideration, the spinster Éponine laments her unrequited love … and all these songs, each with a separate melody, are sung one after the other. Even the chorus joins in, adding layers of depth and intensity to the music. And then something unexpected happens. While, at the start, the characters sing separately, suddenly the voices fuse, singing over each other, until at last they are all singing together: fourteen characters and many contrasting melodies gradually converge, until right at the last minute they all become one sole voice and song. It's breathtaking: the energy of the song 'One Day More' is indescribable.[24]

A selfie world focused only on ourselves has only one heart song: our own. In contrast, seeing the lives of others means trying to discover their voice, their heart song, their truth. It means learning to listen to each other. And there's no doubt that this enriches our own individual dance through life. May the music continue!

---

24. I recommend watching this part of the musical in the version produced to mark its tenth anniversary at the Royal Albert Hall. Although it lacks the mobility of the theatre production, it allows you clearly to discern the voices coming together as one as I've tried to explain: http://bit.ly/1o92o60.

Part Three

10

Feel the Fear

It is rightly said that success has many friends, and failure rather fewer. Only when things go wrong do you discover who your true friends are. The successful immediately find that a wide social circle springs up around them, full of smiling people, tempting career opportunities, glittering invitations, telephone calls, words of praise and adulation. However, when you fail, when difficult times come and your luck is on the downturn, many of these fair-weather friends abandon you without a second thought. This experience of failure can be very solitary, and not only because friends abandon you. It's also a challenge to keep your head held high. You may feel shame at failing or you might be afraid that you don't know how to get out of the hole you've fallen into.

Chapter 15 of Luke's Gospel narrates perhaps the best known parable of the Gospels, with the exception of the Good Samaritan: the story of the Prodigal Son. Most of us know the story of the hedonistic, impulsive young man who asks his father to give him his inheritance in advance, because all he cares about is the present moment. Once he has the money, he leaves without a backward glance. He then splashes out on revelry, parties and hedonism. If St Luke were writing about him today, he'd easily find plenty of settings for his wild, hedonistic night life. In a modern setting, perhaps this lad's problems might start with a message that he had no credit left on his card. It would get worse when he couldn't pay his bills or loans, and would end with him being abandoned by all his party friends. According to the parable, this rebellious lad finds doors shutting, and he slides into a downward spiral until he reaches rock bottom and is hired to feed pigs, while he himself goes hungry, longing to feast on the pigs' pathetic leftovers. It's easy to imagine how crushed and despairing he feels. He might burst into tears, or feel incredulous about his lot, or explode with rage. Most of the time, however, he'd probably be in despair ... and feel very alone.

A dreadful silence, when you feel utterly abandoned and blame yourself, characterises the loneliness of failure. It starts with a lingering self-reproach, echoing inside you. Or with futile tears over your bad luck, the wrong decisions you've made, or the unfortunate situation that sucked you into this downward spiral. To top all this, you worry that that you'll have a breakdown from which you won't recover. Thus, you feel imprisoned by your failure and utterly defeated.

It is also possible to change your tune. Here, the parable gives us two fascinating key insights. The first concerns recovering the blessings of your past. The young man in the parable, who was once so happy to live just in the present, who today would perhaps have used the phrase *carpe diem* on his Twitter profile, begins in the midst of failure to see his past as a source of wisdom. He thinks about whether it has anything of value to teach him in his present situation, and then he lands on the truth: he remembers that in the house of his father even the day labourers were well looked after. I'm sure that memory brings his father to mind, only now he sees him with other eyes: as a tender, concerned and generous father. However, he has a choice: if he follows the path he's chosen in the past, he will remain stuck, trapped in an impossible situation. His great breakthrough is being open to the future: 'I will pick myself up, I will go to my father, and I will say ... ,' he decides. And his focus on the future turns into a plan and a source of hope, which gives him the strength to pick himself up and begin his journey towards the future. This story – or rather all our stories – offers a great heart song to help us cope with the loneliness that dominates certain times in our lives. It's helpful to see every situation that befalls us – through the broadest possible lens – as stages on our journey through life. Doing so will strengthen us and give us a sense of purpose.

The second insight offered by the Prodigal Son parable is about having the humility to acknowledge that sometimes we need to ask for help. That's not easy. Failure can lead us to focus on ourselves, and to say, with a blend of shame and pride, 'If I've fallen down it's up to me to pick myself up again.' That's often like trying to scrape yourself off the floor by the scruff of your neck. If you have no other source of support, however much you try, all you will manage to do is hurt yourself. Other people need to help you to get up. The Prodigal Son recalls in his loneliness the one person who can help him: the good father who loves him and who is doubtless waiting for him. He therefore dares to ask for help – his action in musical terms might be compared to an overture that will segue into a brand-new opera.

If we go yet further into the parable of the Prodigal Son, we discover an intriguing second story which contrasts with the first. There is an older brother who's always been at home and who is indignant at the reception his father gives his crazy little brother when he returns home full of regret for the past. The older son, it emerges, also has his own issues with being alone, which only surface now when he is indignant. When he blows his top with his father over what's happened, everything he's suffered in silence and has been holding in, perhaps for years, pours out: 'All these years I've been slaving for you and never disobeyed your orders,' he says, 'Yet you never gave me even a young goat so I could celebrate with my friends.' That sentence holds a whole universe of pain and loneliness. The boy has silenced his pain, brooding over how he feels his father loves his younger brother more than him. Perhaps the father has looked sad for years, mourning the absence of his younger son. All this time, the older boy kept quiet about his feelings of being unloved. The father's astonished reply, ' 'My son, you are always with me, and everything I have is yours,' might be expressed in other words: 'You only needed to ask.' Now let's imagine what might have happened if, at any point during his inner Calvary, the older son had trusted his father and opened up to him. What if he had lowered his guard, revealed the pain behind his apparent calmness, told his father that he felt alone and asked for a sign of affection? His father, in all likelihood, would have replied with words such as these: 'My son, me not love you? I love you so much and will always love you.' And in this dialogue, in that hurt question and that tender reply, the older son in all his fragility would have found all the celebrations he thought he had been denied.

In our society there is a fear of showing that we're vulnerable. Perhaps we have too much of a hero complex. Many people seem always ready to help others, which is no bad thing, yet are apparently never willing to be helped, which is not good. I don't believe that the world is split into rescuers and victims. After all, we have two hands: one with which to offer help and the other with which to receive it. All too often the giving of help becomes a dynamic that is one-sided – which is sometimes inevitable – but it is rarely received by those who give, which is somewhat worse.

The Prodigal Son shows courage when he throws himself into his father's arms, admitting his past mistakes and his need for help and shelter. This reflects well on him. The younger son could be a good example for any one of us during difficult times when we turn inwards, feeling that it is not worth the hassle to share our hurt and pain with others, as though the world needs us only when we're invulnerable and psychologically intact. Those who love us also need us to be vulnerable and show our limitations; we just need to trust them, to let them give us a hand, and to share with them at least some of our deepest anxieties and problems. Often, as the saying goes, a problem shared is a problem halved. When we share our problems, we feel lighter. Having someone else's perspective can help us to see that the issues weighing us down are actually part of a bigger picture. Sometimes we just need a hug, which is worth more than words, or a friend to help us laugh at ourselves. There's a space for this to happen when, instead of shutting others out, we let others know about our problems.

Part Three

11

You're Magnificent

Countless Gospel stories show Jesus coming close to the untouchables as he goes about his daily life. They're untouchable not in the sense of being part of an overprivileged elite whose status protects them from any form of attack – like a football player whose coach can never criticise him, or a millionaire who is untouchable due to her fortune and army of lawyers. Here the word 'untouchable' quite literally means people others want to keep at a distance. Those whom others hope never to be physically close to, let alone mingle with. 'Untouchable' in this sense means being a pariah pushed to the edge of society.

The 'untouchables' who met Jesus comprised every kind of sinner and invalid, but perhaps the best example of these excluded groups were the lepers. They, more than any other group, were kept at a distance from others. They had to ring a bell as they approached so that people knew they were close by and had time to get away and avoid contact with them. They lived far away from cities. The religious outlook of the time, which made an explicit link between one's circumstances in life and God's decisions, suggested this disease could only be the consequence of behaviour deserving of punishment – either the lepers' acts or those of their ancestors. Whatever the case, lepers were thought to deserve neither clemency nor salvation.

Yet we observe how Jesus time and again in his encounters with lepers does the unthinkable: he touches them. This gesture turns the established order upside down. Some caresses are a silent revolution. Those of Jesus certainly were. That's one reason why he was such a contentious character for the moral watchdogs of his day.

So what is Jesus' message when he encounters each leper? Basically, just the one: 'You are not untouchable.' Quite the contrary. He is saying to them, 'You are worthy of physical affection and respect, of recognition and second chances. You're worthwhile and you can have a place in society.' The lepers' healing therefore does not become a denial of what they were in the past. It is rather an acceptance of them just as they are. Yet their healing also expresses the change and personal growth that occur in all our lives.

Feeling unwanted or worthless or that you have to change your personality to fit in with the demands of a group or the values of a society that excludes others, is at the root of a great deal of contemporary loneliness. For example, many people become martyrs to their 'image'. By this I mean an image that exalts youth, beauty and being slim, yet stigmatises ageing, ugliness (not even that, really, but looking normal) and being fat as undesirable. Many people feel paralysed and destroyed by their insecurity over not attaining these standards, or are distraught about their weight. Combined with the ensuing fear of rejection, this is a complete minefield for many. The word 'image' as used here includes other demands, for example financial status linked to our self-worth, or adhering to group think, whether ideological, political or religious. Often this isn't truly about fidelity to the creed of a given group, but adhering only to fashionable 'on-trend' opinions about problems or conflicts. 'Image' is about doing anything to fit in with the crowd, so you're not tagged as anti-social or weird.

There's a double temptation when you feel like this. The first is accepting being excluded, ostracised and rejected because you feel you deserve it. You feel that this is all your fault, and you don't even try to leave the isolated state in which others have left you. That's the first temptation: to give in. The second temptation is evasion: to lie or economise with the truth in order to cover up what you're going through, what you feel or who you are. Yet accepting and understanding the truth of who we are is precisely what prepares us for genuine encounters with others.

I would like to share two stories that brilliantly illustrate this: both are contemporary fables. One is a full-length movie, the other a short film. Both have been screened in the cinema in recent years. Both are, in some way, eulogies to freedom, because what they offer is an alternative to the temptations mentioned above. They share a heart song of unconditional love and a lesson in how to see the good in others, which frees those who apparently don't fit in from the trap of isolation. This is exactly what Jesus did with those to whom he opened his arms, offering them the good news. His accepting approach to people could become the heart song of our world.

The first story is a fascinating short film: *The Butterfly Circus*.[25] It is set in the 1930s in the US. The Great Depression has left America feeling low. Life in the countryside is harsh and grey. Will – played by the excellent Nick Vujicic, who in real life has no limbs – has neither arms nor legs. He's an exhibit in a travelling circus, the main attraction in the freak show, alongside a bearded lady, a tattooed man and others with physical anomalies. People laugh at Will without mercy. It is not clear how long he has endured this, but long enough for him to have internalised the notion that he is a monster, a freak of nature and that he deserves his lot.

One day a mysterious man visits the freak show. When it's over, he lingers for a minute with Will. Crouching down to Will's height, he says gently, 'You're magnificent.' Will's furious response is to spit in his face. Perhaps this joke feels more painful than the tomatoes that are usually chucked at him. He feels he is grotesque and ugly. Who can call him magnificent with his weird body? It's just not true. Or is it?

The tattooed man, who has witnessed this scene, says to Will when the man leaves, 'Do you know who you just spat it? That's Mr Mendez, the manager of the Butterfly Circus.' (The viewer has to assume that everyone in the freak show knows about the Butterfly Circus, which for some reason has a special significance.) The next thing we know, Will has managed to get someone to help him onto one of the lorries of the Butterfly Circus. When its unusual troupe discover him, they welcome him in, without a second thought. What is quickly apparent is that they are not going to humiliate him. Yet neither do they wrap him in cotton wool. He's just one of the gang. Gradually, Will discovers that Mendez has rescued those who are in the circus from dreadful situations, after

---

25. J. Weigel (director), *The Butterfly Circus*, 2009, http://bit.ly/2wZSBK3.

perceiving in them qualities unseen by anyone else. Mendez has then helped them to discover these qualities in themselves. He has rescued a prostitute from hard times, an old man once abandoned, and an alcoholic who was formerly violent. Will, however, wonders what on earth can be unique, special or lovely about him? He can't seem to find his place, and wonders whether there is really a place for him in the circus or whether he is only going to be a burden. Then one day Mendez pushes him to take a risk while the troupe cross a river; he encourages Will to cross unaided, by wriggling his body over the stones forming a path in the water. Will ends up falling in. At that moment he discovers that although he can't walk, he can swim. His body responds to water and he feels unique.

The circus returns to performing after a break. The main number has everyone on edge. In the middle of the circus ring is a small pool and a post rising right to the top of the circus tarpaulin. That's where Will is, on a trampoline. From that dizzy height, he jumps, landing squarely in the water, which gently keeps him afloat. The audience applauds enthusiastically. Afterwards, many of the circus-goers want to congratulate Will. They include a woman accompanied by a small boy who is missing a leg and who is walking with difficulty on crutches. The little boy, without saying a word, gives Will a hug. The woman says, 'Thank you.' We understand that by seeing Will, the little boy has found a new hope, and has become aware that he too is lovely, in a unique way. That is the unique and lovely heart song of every life. The challenge for each one of us is to learn how to see both others and ourselves with fresh eyes.

The second film is the Australian movie *Muriel's Wedding*.[26] This might look like just another teen movie about the conflicts among a friendship group. In fact, it's a profound analysis of group pressure and social acceptance, the difficulties of fitting in and how to find your own place in the world.

Muriel lives in a boring town called Porpoise Spit. Her father, an ambitious politician, can't stand any of his children, whom he judges to be

---

26. J. Moorhouse and L. House (producers) and P. J. Hogan (director), *Muriel's Wedding*, Film Victoria, 1994.

lazy and failures. Her quiet, resigned mother is quashed by him. Muriel's friends are good-looking, popular, blonde, wear the latest clothes and listen to the latest music. Muriel is fat and feels ugly, and only finds relief while listening to Abba. She dreams of being a success. But what does success really mean? For Muriel it means being like everyone else. Being part of the group. Keen to believe that she belongs, she tries to fool herself until her friends throw her out of the group, telling her some harsh truths: 'You're ugly', 'You're fat', 'You're unpopular', 'And you listen to Abba', they blurt out forcefully, determined to persuade Muriel she doesn't belong.

From that moment on, Muriel sets out to succeed, to fit in with the girls. So she changes her name (because she hates Muriel) and calls herself Mariel. She runs away to Sydney. The odd thing is that she begins to surround herself with people who do genuinely seem to care for her, including her friend Rhonda and her sort-of boyfriend, Brice. Both really like her just as she is. However, driven by her desire to be a success, Mariel agrees to a marriage of convenience with a rich South African swimmer who needs to marry an Australian woman in order to compete in the Olympics.

Her dream wedding – to which the title of the film refers – becomes a crossroads at which two views on life converge … Mariel's frivolous friends come back, enticed by her newfound aura of riches and popularity and the prospect of appearing in glossy magazines as friends of Mariel. Her father – on the arm of his new partner – is enjoying the attention that is his due as the father of the bride. Everyone who applauds, flatters and fusses over this unreal Mariel is contributing to her game-playing and lies. Meanwhile, in the middle of this monumental deception, the three people who truly do love Mariel feel rejected and hurt by her: her mother arrives after a long bus journey and, once again, is ignored by everyone. Rhonda, who is now ill, sees how Mariel is carrying on, and Brice, who is truly in love with her, is pushed away by the lies and fake wedding.

Will Muriel discover what true friends are? Is she able to stop lying? Who will win the battle – the fake popular Mariel or the real Muriel who adores Abba?

Without revealing the film's ending, I think the key to understanding where freedom is here is to learn from what happens to the insecure, complex-ridden Muriel. How often are we tempted to please other people! How often do we do things because of what they might say, or what they might demand of us? How often do we act to gain their approval or give them what they need? If the truth is ugly, we're tempted to cover it up, and become another version of ourselves, changing in order to meet the expectations of others. The danger with all this is that you can end up stuck in a pattern of deception (and occasionally self-deception) which keeps the real you either isolated behind a mask concealing your insecurities or else dependent on the approval of other people. The tragedy is that all too often we end up begging for love from people who demand we act out of character, but fail to realise that we're truly loved by those who like us just as we are.

This particular heart song is encapsulated by the words 'You're magnificent'. Sometimes we all need someone to help us discover this simple and eternal truth. We are each unique, different and exceptional. A world or community in which everyone was cut from the same cloth and fitted the same mould would be a sad and dreary place indeed.

Part Three

12

Someone Else's Shoes: Judgement and Prejudices

If we were able to put ourselves in another's shoes more often, how different our interactions and personal relationships might be!

There is a passage in the Gospels that is highly instructive about the danger of judging other people when we don't know them. A woman has been caught in adultery and is brought to Jesus by men who want to see what he, the teacher, will say. Her captors surround her expectantly, all set to stone her, as the law dictates, because she is guilty of deceiving her husband and violating the accepted codes of behaviour. We can easily imagine the judgements the men are muttering under their breath: 'She should have thought first', 'She deserves it, the shameless hussy' (and for shameless, replace this with other, less polite phrases), or 'There's no decency nowadays.' In short, it's quite clear that an unassailable barrier, constructed from their judgement and lack of empathy, separates this woman from her accusers. They – who are 'pure', 'perfect' and law-abiding, feel like they are the rightful judges of this unfaithful wife. The only thing they are waiting for is for Jesus to ratify their judgement. They've already filled their hands with stones.

Then, in just one sentence, Jesus unsettles them: 'Let he who is free from sin cast the first stone.' What he means is, 'Has it occurred to you that there might be similarities between your own lives and that of this woman you cast at my feet?' After taking the time to think this through properly, they realise he's right. Who hasn't occasionally crossed a line they once thought written in stone? Who hasn't sometimes let down the people they love? Who hasn't been in that awkward position of having to ask forgiveness because it's the only way back after you've made a mistake? Thoughts akin to this narrow the once yawning gap between the men and the adulterous woman. The stones fall from their hands as, starting with the eldest, they start to walk away.

Putting yourself in someone else's shoes and identifying with them is the way to a different kind of encounter. That's not to say it's easy. It's easier to misinterpret, judge and reject others from a safe distance than learn to recognise that you are equally guilty of the faults you judge in others.

Just think, for instance, of the lack of communication that is so typical in the political world. All too often we see the spokesmen – of any party – attack the inconsistencies of their opponents, but refusing to exercise even a minimum of self-criticism in areas where their party is equally culpable. Quite often this is due not to hypocrisy per se, but rather to our all too frequent habit of seeing the speck in another's eye rather than the log in our own. Thus, between us we put up a barrier through which we view, judge and condemn other people, although the truly sincere and productive approach would involve us being far more transparent about both our own and other people's difficulties in the struggle against corruption and the pitfalls of public life. Unfortunately, however, politics in a democracy is not a shared reflection in order to reach a potential consensus on the truth, but instead a ruthless fight, based on appearances, to obtain votes.

Very often I've had to help people who are going through conflicts: arguing families, friends who have fallen out over an incident where neither one appears to be at fault, employees who feel oppressed in the workplace, or members of religious orders enduring painful conflicts in their communities. Quite frequently in such disagreements, when I've had the chance to listen to both sides, one thing becomes blatantly obvious: if everyone involved were able to put themselves in the other's shoes and, just for a second, understand their circumstances, their motivation and how they are experiencing the situation, then perhaps everything wouldn't be instantly resolved, but at least the defences held on to by each side might start to come down.

The judge Frank Caprio, described in some press outlets as 'the most just judge in the world', has gained a certain popularity in the US and on social media. Judge Caprio has managed to move people through the way he leads his sessions in court. While these involve everyday judgments for minor infractions, the way in which he addresses people, his empathy as he tries to understand their situation and resolve the cases concerned have made him a popular, inspiring figure. About twenty years ago, his brother started to film him in action to show how the courtroom can become a place of profound encounter and not just an arena of demands or conflict. Today, these videos have been turned into the documentary show, *Caught in Providence*, which has really taken off on social media, allowing thousands of people to discover Judge Caprio's extremely humane approach to treating others as our neighbour.[27]

It is absolutely essential that we learn how to put ourselves in other people's shoes, instead of dividing the world into saints and sinners. There is a terrible temptation to take a Manichæistic world view. When you divide the world into the pure and the impure, my people and others, what you end up with is a black-and-white picture of the world scarred by inflexible, divisive borders, where we are prepared to throw stones at anyone who dares to think, act or opine differently from us. When we take the time to perceive nuances, to listen to each other and find the similarities we share with others, we create a common ground for future productive and mutual encounters.

Judgement is what drives the men in the Gospel story who were ready to stone the adulteress, but prejudice also appears endlessly in the Gospels, whenever a person is defined by a label without ever being given the chance to show their individual quirks, their human qualities or their depth. Many people appear under a label in the Gospels: Romans, publicans, Samaritans, tax-collectors, prostitutes, lepers, shepherds, Galileans, the people of Nazareth ... time and again we see how Jesus' behaviour is always breaking down the preconceptions that define his society. When

---

[27]. The programmes may be seen on various channels but this is the link to the YouTube episodes. Each has a common thread of compassion, common sense and a desire to help people in their particular situations: http://bit.ly/2ezoXUw.

we label people in our society and can't get beyond pigeonholing people, we're lost. It's so easy to label others! Occasionally, it is even necessary, because social labels help us to find our place, and give us a key to interpret what is happening in society. They can also guide us through social minefields.

The problem arises when we operate solely and wholly via labelling others and start to classify people as friends or enemies according to our experiences, tastes or upbringing. This is how we pigeonhole others in either a positive or a negative light. A while ago I wrote the following text which is also highly relevant here:

> Let's play at breaking down a few stereotypes. Not everyone on the Right is a fascist. Neither are all those on the Left hippies or jobsworths. Being a bureaucrat doesn't necessarily mean that you barely do a jot of work. Not all Andalusians live off the state. Not all priests are pederasts. Neither are all bishops fuddy-duddies. Not all politicians are corrupt. Not all trade unionists are cheeky. Not all Catalans are stingy. Not everyone in the political party you support is honourable, nor is everyone in any other party a flake. Not every gay is promiscuous. Neither are all gays sensitive and noble. Not every decision of the political party you sympathise with is correct or timely. Nor are all those from the party you can't stand, idiotic. The young, simply because of their youth, are not necessarily more committed, generous or caring than older people. For the same reason, neither are they lazier, more frivolous or more superficial. Not every Madrileño is born and bred in Madrid. Not every entrepreneur exploits his employees. Nor are all workers the victims of a class system, just as not every businessman is an energetic job creator. Nor are all salaried staff lazy and only bothered about their time off. Not everyone who watches TV is stupid. Nor are all blondes dumb (and many aren't real blondes either). Not every Asturian is affable. Neither is every person from Valladolid cold.

> I say, down with labels! Down with simplistic prejudices and pigeon-holing other people! Life is subtle and complex. Each of us is unique and full of quirks.[28]

If only we were able to learn for once and for all that while others differ from us we also resemble each other far more than we realise. Learning this would open the way for so many genuine encounters with each other. It's far more tempting to build barriers between us and other people, to throw stones at them from the interior castle we retreat to, rather than trying to understand their motivation and outlook and what we actually share in common. When we manage to free ourselves from this pattern of excluding and pre-judging others, this heart song of our encounters thrives with possibility! This might include encounters with those who don't think like us, who have standards we don't share, or who have ideas that are the polar opposite of our own, or they might have a different experience or outlook on life from ours. Such encounters are beneficial because they make us engage with each other from a starting place of difference rather than being the same, which is dull and boring.

---

28. J. M. Rodríguez Laizola, *Mosaico Humano,* Santander: Sal Terrae, 2015, p. 33.

13

You Need to Start Taking Yourself Seriously

Resentment and blame make disquieting travelling companions. Both are extremely isolating. Both are extreme ends of the emotional journey we go through whenever we are hurt. Then, both the victim and the perpetrator may be affected by what has happened. Victims are imprisoned by their own resentment. Perpetrators, if able to realise what they have done and are repentant, are imprisoned by their guilt.

St Peter's tears early on the morning of Good Friday are one of the most moving scenes in the Gospels. Peter has just spectacularly let down his best friend, the teacher whom he had sworn to protect with his life, if necessary. When the moment of truth comes, he is in the grip of fear and tension. Every time he is asked to step forward, to side with the accused, condemned Jesus, Peter denies having anything to do with him.

In one account of that fateful night, there is even a moment where Jesus and Peter exchange a glance, in a speechless instant of recognition, of naked truth. When, shortly afterwards, the cock crows, Peter weeps, realising how much he has betrayed Jesus, as Jesus had predicted only hours earlier. He weeps with sorrow, anguish and regret. He weeps with guilt, and he weeps alone, just as we cry our most bitter and shameful tears, those we cannot contain, alone.

The loneliness of guilt is very tough, because it is rooted in a fragility laid bare, in the experience of having messed up, of having let down God, failed ourselves or let down someone we love, which, perhaps, is what causes us the most anxiety. Obviously we're upset when we mess up on our own, but we always can say that we have no choice but to live with and accept our mistakes. When we have let God down, we know, even in the midst of our contrariness and self-torture, that God is a God of mercy. We learn to trust that, however often we abandon and desert him, he keeps his hand outstretched towards us through thick and thin. But what of those we let down although we love them? What enormous pain we suffer for having hurt them, for having failed to meet their expectations, kept our promises or perhaps behaved as they hoped we would. Guilt is a source of torment, of sleepless nights, where you go over and over again in your mind things that could have been otherwise. Guilt paralyses and disturbs us. It may bring us to the brink of exhaustion. It confronts us with the prospect of trying to rectify matters and find new ways forward.

If the perpetrator experiences the loneliness of guilt, the loneliness induced by resentment which sometimes takes hold of victims is equally painful – if not more so. It's never easy to bear the burden of what we suffer at the hands of others. The world today knows many forms of abuse and violence. Due to this, we should not speak too lightly of forgiveness without an awareness of the wounds people suffer because of violence, rejection, every form of abuse, exclusion, betrayal, lies, apathy and exploitation. All this is happening in our world, and it leaves people damaged and wounded.

Anyone who feels they are a victim and is wounded by an attack, offence, grievance or disappointment may end up imprisoned by their hatred. Resentment may give us the strength to carry on, even to pursue revenge, but, more often than not, it eats you up inside. It locks you into your wounded memories, where, even without wanting to, you end up giving your attacker the ultimate victory – of imprisoning you in spite and bitterness. And it really is a prison, because you end up making that very person or people who you should perhaps pay least attention to, the centre of your world. Living stuck in resentment is also a very solitary experience.

In the case of guilt and resentment, the heart song that changes everything is forgiveness. This entails taking a perspective that is able to see beyond hatred and guilt, whether that is forgiveness that is asked for or that is granted. As a melody from the heart, forgiveness is not easy, but delicate, subtle and complicated. But it is possible.

Tango for One

Some people have testimonies of indescribable beauty which show us how to confront inner torment in astonishing ways. Their words become poetry for us, a source of hope.

This is true of the inner world of Etty Hillesum, who lived through the hell of Nazi Germany as a Jew. She spent her final years in a transit camp for Eastern Europe, knowing that she would probably end up on one of the trains that always left full and always returned empty. In fact, she died at Auschwitz. She endured the rudeness of the Gestapo, and heard her fellow Jews weep, their complaints turning into a desire for vengeance. Yet Etty, out of her deep passion for life and sense of universal communion with the rest of humanity, expressed through her letters and her diary the essence of forgiveness. She had the freedom that wells up within, whenever people discover inside themselves the strength, hope and greatness of spirit necessary to resist giving in to hate. In doing so, they show us that it is possible.

> We may of course be sad and depressed by what has been done to us; that is only human and understandable. However: our greatest injury is one we inflict upon ourselves. I find life beautiful and I feel free. The sky within me is as wide as the one stretching above my head. I believe in God and I believe in man, and I say so without embarrassment. Life is hard, but that's no bad thing. If one starts by taking one's own importance seriously, the rest follows. It is not morbid individualism to work on oneself. True peace will come only when every individual finds peace within himself; when we have all vanquished and transformed our hatred for our fellow human beings of whatever race – even into love one day, although perhaps that is asking too much. It is, however, the only solution.[29]

'If one starts by taking one's own importance seriously, the rest follows,' said Etty. Is that a display of self-sufficiency? Do we not also learn

---

29. Etty Hillesum, *An Interrupted Life: The Diaries 1941–1943 and Letters from Westerbork*, New York, NY: Henry Holt and Company, 1996, pp.144–45.

forgiveness from God? Do others not matter, whether they be perpetrators or victims in conflicts?

I think we need to get a grip on what this passionate, brilliant woman is saying. What she is referring to is a change of outlook: the recognition that each of us has our own inner world, and is called to salvage the radical dignity that we value so highly, whenever we need to take the first step.

This dignity means that sometimes we are able to forgive and keep going forward. At other times, it teaches us to ask for forgiveness – and accept that we may or may not receive it. Sometimes, the loneliness of our resentment and guilt creates an abyss that engulfs us on all sides. It is an abyss caused by our failures and the times we disappoint each other, an abyss made from our blame or fear. Taking ourselves seriously, therefore, means discovering that we have the way out of the abyss within us. It's within our power to choose or reject this path out of danger. We can take that path towards the perpetrator, or the victim (depending on which one we are), or we may just keep walking in any direction we need to in order to carry on living without staying stuck in the horror of our memory.

Yet when we refer to victims of any kind of pain who may well have a thousand reasons to make hatred or resentment their rationale, what does it mean for them to take themselves seriously? It means not handing over power to the person who has victimised you so that you effectively let them keep you captive while they hold the last card: their repentance. Perhaps they will never repent, nor realise what they've done to you. However, your innate dignity does not depend on their regret. To take oneself seriously is to remember that it is not the victim but rather the one who attacks, abuses or strikes the innocent party who lacks dignity. The words 'Father, forgive them, for they do not know what they do' is the finest expression of this freedom. It means believing that your wounds too can heal. It means accepting that you can always shift from resentment to indifference, from indifference to forgiveness and from forgiveness to being open to whatever the future may bring.

When we refer to those at the opposite end of the scale who are imprisoned in their guilt, what does taking yourself seriously mean for them?

It means giving oneself permission to carry on, to get beyond the sense of resignation and failure you feel on being obliged to face your own mediocrity. It means accepting your own weakness. This does not mean, however, casually justifying bad behaviour with the argument that we are all fragile. It is rather the acceptance of your own vulnerability – the daring to look at yourself in the mirror although you may not like what you see there. Taking yourself seriously means daring to ask for pardon, but accepting that you may not receive it. It means truly believing that you can be a better person if you can manage to transform your repentance into a touchstone that will guide your future behaviour.

In this context, I imagine the dance as akin to that of a soloist on an empty stage. All the other dancers have vanished. The soloist's body lies motionless on the floor – frozen by its own mistakes or by the wounds inflicted by others. At first, there is no movement at all. Everything feels heavy, as though perhaps the recumbent dancer is waiting for someone to come along and pick them up – but no one comes. However, in the end, the body starts to move. A hand is raised, an arm stirs, the torso straightens and the dance begins, hesitantly at first and then with an intense energy.

We must find our victory within ourselves, in that strength – which believers call the Holy Spirit – that lights a fire deep within us. No one can demand forgiveness of us nor oblige us to forgive, but when we allow this spirit of concord, reconciliation and forgiveness (whether of ourselves or others) to come in, then we are transformed into a brilliant likeness of the God of encounters.

Part Three

14

Dancing with Death

You might be shocked by the title of this chapter, because we tend to represent death – on the rare occasions that we do so – as a hooded skeleton, bearing a scythe who appears only to bring desolation and loss. However, that's not necessarily the truth. In Chapter 6 I referred to the wound of death, how death is hidden in the modern world, and how, by virtue of silencing death, its impact is all the more deafening when it comes, especially if it is unexpected or premature.

Through his humanity, God did not free himself from death (and death on the Cross). In this universal and final experience all that was most vulnerable about Jesus himself was at stake, and his friends, however much they did not want to, had to accept his death. And while it's true that faith gives us the hope of resurrection or life after death, it is none the less also true that when death comes, we have to process and cope with it first in the darkness, in desperation, like that first Holy Saturday when it seemed that the tomb of Christ was irrevocably sealed. Often we too have to go through that time of uncertainty and unknowing, although we may be able to live open to hope.

What does it mean to dance with death? It means learning to see it not as an enemy, but rather as a travelling companion which, at some stage, we will all meet. It means seeing death as a familiar presence, which, when it occurs periodically in our lives, becomes our teacher.

I remember some older relations of my grandmother who would often laugh and joke as they read the death notices in the newspaper. They weren't nasty or insensitive. It was just that they had lived through situations that had made them laugh at death as though mocking a travelling companion of long acquaintance. They had lost loved ones in the

Spanish Civil War and the difficult post-war years in Spain and they understood that our time on earth is limited. So because they knew many people whose names appeared in the death notices, they remembered their time with them in cheerful, jolly tones. Death, in this context, was neither a tragedy nor an inconvenience but rather a reminder to be grateful for times past.

Death, when we are able to contemplate it serenely, can teach us many things: how to value life as a marvellous gift; to enjoy each day as a present; to appreciate the time we are able to share with our loved ones; not to leave words unsaid; not to make mountains out of molehills. It also teaches us that tears are part of love. We shouldn't be afraid to weep for those we love, because the real tragedy would be not to feel their passing. Death forces us to grasp that although we love those who are no longer with us, we don't lose our memories of them, the times we shared and what we achieved together. That all forms part of our emotional inheritance, which no one can take from us. It also teaches us to appreciate our nearest and dearest, for while we are sharply aware of the loss of a loved one who has died, we also know that we who are left behind still need each other. Perhaps all we can do for the deceased is to pray for them and say farewell. Life carries on, as we encounter new people and experiences who will take their place in our personal story.

A few years ago, a curious fact was published in the press; according to the records, the oldest man in the world in August 2017 was 112 years old and was from Extremadura in western Spain. This made me reflect on how each generation passes on the baton of life. Did this man ever think about the fact that all the people alive the year he was born were already dead by 2017? The day will come when all of us here on earth now will be gone, but life, history, human talent and genius will carry on. Life is like a race in which we pass on the baton to the next generation. Perhaps that baton passing is marked by a defining moment: death. This too is a 'dance'. We build things, we love, we write, we sing, we sow, we reap, we imagine, but at the end of the day we have to leave all these things for others to continue in our wake. That feeling that we are part of a greater stream of life, a mere thread in the solid rope of human history, is immensely liberating.

Death reminds us, flying in the face of the world's all-too-deceptive discourse, that the span of our life is limited. It also teaches us to fight for life, just when we discover that we can never take it for granted, to fight against more premature, unnecessary or innocent deaths. We should work to avoid many of the deaths that devastate us today in so many places in the world, and we should also keep trusting that doctors and scientific researchers will continue their efforts to challenge every life-threatening evil. However, I don't think their aim should be to make life last for ever, but rather to better human life so that we can take full advantage of our time on earth.

Death leads us to reflect deeply on life, its meaning and its significance, sparking questions that push us to find answers. From a spiritual perspective, death opens us to resurrection. That does not make our farewells any less painful, but it does offer fresh hope to the believer.

At the end of the day, death comes to us all, either with trumpet blast or in silence, unforeseen or heralded with ample time for us to say our goodbyes. That farewell will always involve an element of liturgy, a dose of insecurity and a measure of dancing.

Part Four

Encounters

Now we're ready to go into the world of encounters, a step beyond the reasons for loneliness, and identifying the best tools and heart song to cope with this. One fascinating aspect of the Gospels is their focus on a continuous experience of community. Jesus calls his disciples to live and work together. He always sends them out together. A group of men and women, whom he will eventually call 'friends', congregates round him. He speaks to them of gathering in his name. He connects them.

The community of Jesus is not unrealistic, pastoral or idyllic, composed of pure souls living in perfect harmony. It is a group of real people, with all their qualities and failings, who love each other but who also argue; who sometimes celebrate together and sometimes have fierce arguments, whether they're fighting over who takes first place, where their money is going or how they understand their mission. They are just people who have to learn how to get along with each other amid day-to-day pressures, in times of celebration and success, but also in times of fear and failure. The lovely thing is that what unites them is more important than what separates them. When, in those wobbly early days of the emerging Church, we meet the disciples of Jesus, still insecure and not really clear about their mission, we see them together in Jerusalem, hidden, but together in danger, praying together, hiding together, in a house filled with friends, a mother and women who follow Jesus and who have become a community.

I believe that the true experience of community and of belonging lies in seeking and sometimes finding things with other people. It's about having to learn as you go along. It's not about smooth relationships that always flow harmoniously, but rather relationships that sometimes flow and at other times get stuck, but where those involved are always learning how to grow.

A few years ago, the film *La Grande Bellezza* (The Great Beauty, 2013)[30] took film festivals around the world by storm. It's an edgy story whose sceptical take on humanity some might find disturbing. It's a story of decadence, nostalgia, banality and the beauty we discern at certain points in our lives. The film's early scenes feature a dance taking place at the main character's birthday party. That scene, set on a luxurious balcony in Rome to the sound of music by Raffaella Carrà, manages to convey both loneliness and encounter. It depicts people making desperate efforts to belong to the group, to find – just for a moment – that they are welcome, accepted, part of the gang, yet this emotion is leavened with the contrasting image of people looking hurt and, in their silence, looking as though they've given up.

Part of what makes us human is our life together and how we interact with each other. Most of us are not by nature hermits, keen to live as far apart from other people as possible. The opposite is true: we need each other, we search for each other, we get to know each other, we love each other and sometimes we're afraid of each other.

Elsewhere in this book, I've mentioned situations where, for one reason or another, communication breaks down, our links become tenuous or our paths no longer meet.

This isn't the place to go further into problems. So I'd like to take a look instead at our options. We all have the chance to belong to groups, communities or families, and this experience shapes who we are, even if we're not always aware of this. Community begins with encounter. When two or more people identify with each other and love each other, they become for others a place of celebration and refuge, an open house.

Saying that, I don't want to set the bar too high. I'm not trying to describe communities that are so ideal, or relationships that are so idyllic or interactions that are so perfect that most people would regard them askance (and perhaps with a touch of envy) as something quite alien.

---

30. N. Giuliano and F. Cima (producers) and P. Sorrentino (director), *La Grande Bellezza*, Medusa Films, 2013, https://bit.ly/32S7YkI.

That's simply not our day-to-day experience. Our families tend not to have high-faluting spiritual or intellectual conversations or swap thoughts on the meaning of life the way people do in films. Our religious communities are not typically havens of peace and beatific co-existence. In our friendship groups there are misunderstandings and tricky situations, people let each other down or don't understand each other. There are careless words and wounding silences. Marriages are not always the perfect union of two people who match each other so perfectly that the only thing left is for them to share their joy with others. Yet, despite all this, we still want to be with each other. We still need each other. And we learn how to stay together. These communities give us roots, form our support network and help us to live the way we do.

It is profoundly human to categorise other people in order to find out who we are. We are all constantly forming groups, either through affection, or shared tastes – because we think the same way or share the same beliefs – or through our nationality, interests, or even just due to coincidence. The truth is we want to meet each other.

15

My Tribe

Sometimes I think that each one of us has our own heart song. It's just that we don't realise this because we've gone deaf. It exists, all the same, and if we manage to tune in to each other, we can share mutual experiences and connections, not only with our nearest and dearest but even with the people we normally keep at a distance.

Sometime we don't even realise how many groups we belong to, or how many links we've formed with other people, and the vast possibility this offers us for real encounter. I'm not referring to ideal, perfect meetings, based on potential affinities. I mean those casual day-to-day encounters that are nothing extraordinary, and may be just passing, yet which may turn into a chat, a shared joke or bit of banter.

11 July 2010 was a very special day in Spain. After an intense world championship full of unforgettable moments, Andrés Iniesta's goal at the end of extra-time following an agonising match in South Africa ensured that Spain became the football world champions. For a few minutes, people in Spain stopped whatever they were doing. The streets filled with people wearing red. The beeping of car horns was music to our ears. Hordes of people flocked outside en masse to celebrate the victory. In cities, towns, streets and squares, bars and cafés, people greeted each other with excitement. Old and young, men and women of every ideological belief, social class or opinion came together. Obviously, a few people chose to remain on the margins, but most people, for just a few moments, lowered their guard. Whether they knew each other nor not, for a few days everyone danced together with joy.

Understandably, this collective enthusiasm dissipated over the course of the summer. Had it been an illusion all along? Or imaginary? No. It was real. It's just that it couldn't possibly last. Daily routines quickly re-emerged and so did the usual fault lines and fights between different groups. However, I still sometimes remember that first magical night of celebration and shared happiness as a snapshot of the chances we truly have to encounter each other. Ultimately, this wasn't really about football – which at the end of the day is ephemeral – it was moment of mutual shared happiness, a brief spurt of crazy celebration at a point when Spain was struggling through a tough economic crisis. It was an excuse not to talk of what so often divides us. This was a very normal feeling of satisfaction with our victory and it was a source of pride to discover, for once, that we were part of something that united rather than divided us.

At times, loneliness afflicts us because we don't really know who we are or we don't see how to relate to other people because we keep our psychological defences up and are guarded with others. On the other hand, if we lower our guard, even for only a few minutes, we open ourselves up to really meet others. This allows us to see that, just like us, they suffer, weep and love. They too get worked up over nothing. They too have desires they don't dare voice aloud. Perhaps they too are impatient. Perhaps like us, they may display when talking a confidence that they don't really have. Connections or encounters begin when we spend time truly getting to know another.

Sometimes, we're so weighed down by what divides us we don't recognise just how much we have in common. That's when we lay down stringent boundaries separating 'us' from 'them'. From there it's just a short step to saying, 'Go get 'em.' Those words, once used by football fans, are now used to harangue people in politics, over faith or in any conflict in which 'we' are completely in the right and 'they' become the enemy. It can also happen to us in the Church. There are so many reasons for the constant in-fighting that seeing what some Catholics say about others can sometimes make you feel like getting out altogether. With the endless clarifications, objections, reciprocal accusations of intransigence on the one hand and of superficiality on the other, the remarks made in malice, scorn and sometimes even hatred on social media ... it's really easy to feel a bit overwhelmed when faced with so much hardness of heart. Yet what if, just for a moment, we let our guard down? What if, just for a moment, we made space instead to talk of the many things we have in common? What if we recognised that we are united by one faith, one spiritual quest, one way of celebrating – with every possible shade of nuance – the Word that speaks to us all? What if we gave ourselves permission to accept that other people have their reasons for thinking as they do and listening to them might perhaps be an opportunity for us to question our convictions? What a welcome respite for rest and communion this might offer!

This is how we could start to focus on the affinities we have with each other, and a shared sense of belonging that we're not always aware of. What might happen if we applied this to our country, our cities, our Church?

Sometimes opportunities for meeting others are provided not through our belonging to the same group, but through a shared hobby. The potential is endless. Followers of *Game of Thrones* might spend hours discussing their favourite characters. Fans of musicians or singers who know their recordings off by heart might get stuck into discussing their best and worst hits. Bibliophiles who adore a certain author and have read all their books may spend hours recalling memorable passages of their *oeuvre*. Anyone who has completed the Camino de Santiago might enjoy meeting other ex-pilgrims with whom to swap memories of those magic days. Foodies familiar with the tasting menus of a particular region might describe their favourite dishes to each other in a wealth of a detail. Video gamers might be impatient for the release of a new, groundbreaking version of a video game. Others may find volunteering an enriching pastime, or own dogs, or love climbing or salsa dancing. The list could go on for ever. There are so many hobbies that have the potential to be a place of encounter, and none is superfluous.

Personally I like the image of the clan, group or tribe: big, sometimes huge groups, which are complex and diverse, in which we're united by similarities that are more important that our differences, where we share common traits and learning experiences together even when we're not aware of doing so. On our journey through life, we encounter each other in many and very often broad social settings. What's really sad is when we fail to notice what we have in common, or when we don't value or appreciate how much even the most casual rapport may bring us.

We must be careful, however, of the ever-present risk of turning our tribe into a sect. This happens whenever we get into the harmful pattern of shutting ourselves off in exclusive social circles, or if we build our identity on rejecting those who are different, or if our prejudices are stronger than our willingness to encounter others. When we do this, we all fall into the trap of closing ourselves off from each other.

Yet, when we're able to navigate these dangers, when familiarity protects us without isolating us, and gives us an identity that does not mean rejecting others, when it defines but doesn't limit us, then a sense of belonging, which may encompass many quite diverse elements, becomes an essential form of support for the journey we make – or even dance – with others.

Part Four

16

Your People

What I've been trying to say up until now is that this initial sense of belonging to a group, while it may fulfil many of our needs, is not, however, something so demanding, exclusive, unique or intimate as to be possible only within two or three relationships, friendships or romantic relationships. While this connection may bring us many experiences, it may not fulfil us as much as the special relationship we have with just a few people.

In other words, you can also create close-knit circles of friends that are so special to you, and belonging to them so important, that you can't imagine life without them. That's where our true friends, family, spouses or partners – any relationship, in short, that you chose to cultivate, fits in.

I'd like now to share a few reflections on these important, necessary relationships, which, if they let us down, may spark increasing feelings of loneliness. I refer to this group as 'my people', because they are the people with whom you feel safe, protected and at home. We each probably have our own list of 'my people'. These are relationships worth cultivating, indulging in and working on so that they may become a home and a refuge for us.

Five elements appear to be essential when it comes to cultivating these relationships so that they reveal their heart song: gratuitousness, generosity, acceptance, freedom and perspective. I'll try to explain each one in turn.

1. *Gratuitousness*

One of the great dangers we face in our key relationships is slipping into a mentality of negotiation. When we overthink who is giving what in our relationships, it may lead to rigidity. When everything needs to be reciprocated, and when we start to calculate who in a relationship is contributing or giving the most, who calls more, who writes most, it is like to choosing a dynamic of compensation instead of gratuitousness. This involves being willing to do your part without demanding anything in return. It means accepting that relationships may be uneven. It means refusing to build relationships on the basis that everything we give is calculated so that, when the time comes, we may claim due recompense.

But is this possible? Or even desirable? Can a relationship work when one person gives everything and the other nothing? Isn't this just opening the door to abuse, to tolerating another person being selfish and self-centred? To answer this, we need to get a proper understanding of what gratuitousness truly is. It's not about being someone who always gives their all only to find the other person never responds. That really isn't helpful in either friendships or romantic relationships. The only context where such an imbalance might possibly be sustained is in the radical, persevering love of parents whose children are recalcitrant egotists who respond to love only with endless demands. However, gratuitousness does not involve a complete lack of proportion. It is about deciding to never give in a calculating fashion, nor keep a tally, but instead accepting that we're all different, and therefore all have different ways of sharing with and giving to each other. Gratuitousness isn't about never desiring reciprocity from your other half. It is rather about learning how not to demand a response as a prerequisite for offering love yourself.

2. *Generosity*

With this trait, I'd like to emphasise our capacity to give ourselves to others. Egotism makes a poor travelling companion. The egotist ends up alone, even when surrounded by other people. If you only take care of yourself, only ever think of your own convenience, never telephone your friends to see how they are but only because you want something from them, if you only conjugate in the first person singular, need to be the centre of every conversation and story, to have a finger in every pie, to talk always of your own problems but never have time to listen to the problems of others, it's likely that you will end up stuck – as observed in a previous chapter – in a narcissistic world view.

If, on the other hand, you build your relationships on the basis of wanting to know and understand others and to give yourself to them; if you truly discover that, as St Paul says, 'You will be enriched in every way so that you can be generous on every occasion' (2 Corinthians 9: 1); if you manage to grasp that all you have – your talent, joy, heart song, strength (and weakness) is for giving to others; if you learn to live by reaching out to others or allowing them to reach out to you; if you share your time, energy, plans and ideas with others; if you're truly interested in others and make space for them in your world, then you will enjoy true, genuine encounters.

3. Acceptance

'If you love me, love me for my faults, anyone may love me for my virtues,' exclaims a character in Gogol's *Dead Souls*. This decisive statement pinpoints something remarkable. In a world where we're constantly either demanding with others, or else measuring ourselves against them, or judging and evaluating one another, the truth is that we need to know when to take off our masks and let ourselves be seen as we truly are. Naturally, all of us have our private spaces and vulnerabilities that we are too embarrassed to reveal in public because they make us feel exposed. However, when we actually let another into these private spaces, their presence can often prove soothing, even a blessing. Why? What acceptance means is having a regard for others that both accompanies and heals. We shouldn't confuse this with conformity or indifference. Acceptance doesn't mean not caring about anything. It does mean loving the whole person just as they are, with their problems and faults and their quirks, rather than cherry-picking the bits of them we like. If there's a flaw in their character that needs to be addressed, we should never approach this in an accusatory fashion, but rather as part of a shared process of two people growing together and aspiring to be better. The poet Dulce María Loynaz captures this in her fine verse that reads: 'If you love me, love all of me / not just in my parts of light or shadow. / If you love me, love me as both black and white. / And in my greyness, and my green and as a blonde / and as a brunette. / Love me in the day /

Love me in the night ... / And in the morning with the window wide open! ... / If you love me, don't cut me up into different parts / Love all of me ... or don't love me at all!'

4. Freedom

Freedom is essential in deep, meaningful relationships, because love – which is what we're really talking about here – cannot be forced, nor can it be demanded. What is freedom in a relationship? The exact opposite of the carelessness of someone flitting from one partner to another, without any desire to commit to a permanent relationship. In that balance between belonging and freedom lies the touchstone for all our most meaningful relationships.

Some people see any kind of complaint or demand from another person as a restriction or constraint on their freedom. If we live like that, we start to feel overburdened, get a sinking feeling and fear being possessed by our partner or spouses. However, commitment implies giving our spouse licence to have an opinion about our lives. It implies ceding part of our autonomy in order to lay the groundwork for a shared mutual future. It implies thinking less in the singular and more in the plural. Having said this, however, we need to avoid living relationships out of a crazy co-dependency, and a desire to control the other person or meddle constantly with their concerns. This is because freedom is a commitment but never a trap, a bond but never a prison sentence.

So how should we understand freedom? It's the ability to decide with whom and how we wish to bind ourselves in marriage, being fully aware that this choice entails sacrificing some of our autonomy, and involves your other half influencing you, having a say about your decisions, or having an opinion about you. It also involves choosing to share your projects, plans, time and space. In short, marrying is a choice to interact with another rather than living in splendid isolation, and being prepared, once this *pas de deux* begins, to rely on your partner to help you find the way forward in those journeys of the heart that swing from togetherness to temporary retreat.

5. Perspective

Finally, perspective involves being able to understand our relationships as stories in development, rather than brief episodes of joy, intense feeling or moments of fulfilment, connection and satisfaction. All our deepest, most genuine relationships consolidate over time. We learn as we go along. Gaining perspective helps us to learn and acquire wisdom from our experience.

One of the major problems of our fast-paced world is our lack of perspective – we want everything now and have short-term memories because anything long-term seems out of place. This is partly fuelled by the avalanche of news reports featuring public figures who constantly jostle to dominate the public arena. This dynamic, so typical of the media, is speedily invading other areas of life. When it infects our relationships, we're exposed to the tyranny of living only in the deceptive sphere of the here and now. We live at a fast pace and excessively in the present. That's no problem when the *here* is comfortable and the *now* is positive. It may become a problem when we are obliged to live through turbulent times, or seasons of conflict and difficulty.

When, however, you regain perspective and are able to perceive your situation from a greater distance, your sense of belonging, whether to a group or a relationship, can be seen with far more context, in shades of grey rather than black and white. This is when you really can learn from the situation you're in, about yourself, about others and about your relationship as a work in progress. This kind of perspective can help you with making decisions, or even changing direction if, for whatever reason, your relationship stalls. You can remember your purpose at this point, and keep moving forwards towards your dreams. This type of perspective can help you to understand your spouse's decisions and accept their mistakes, so as to survive the rough patches and celebrate golden times with serenity.

17

Dancing Alone

Perhaps it's obvious that occasionally you have to dance alone, at times when neither your tribe nor your people are close by, though they may be around. At such times, it can feel like you are alone and facing the truth of who you are. Learning to know, love and respect oneself is therefore a vital life lesson.

To understand the heart song of the universe and to be in step with others, and with the Other who is God, we also need times of privacy and disconnection, of silence filled with solitude. This occasional silence is a place for reflection, where we put our life in order and gain perspective and a sense of purpose. Our ability to reflect both personally and in the world we inhabit lends greater depth of meaning and essence to who we are. In silence and solitude, we will discover the seed of those talents and attitudes which, at a later point in our life, may bear fruit.

The first such quality is a healthy self-pride. By that, I don't mean arrogance or conceit or superiority. This is actually about being at peace with yourself, because you know that you are unique. We all are. No two people are the same. There's never been anyone just like you, either in the past or now, nor will there be anyone just like you in the future. No one else has your thoughts or has had your upbringing. They don't know the words that shaped your future. They haven't lived where you've lived. They don't have your family or friends. They are not party to your silliest thoughts and most sensible ideas, have not shed your tears, or shared the laughs that brightened your days. They have never received the same declarations of love as you or known your inner turmoil. They haven't had to make the decisions you needed to make, or known of the choices you have not managed to make. They have never attained your particular successes nor made your unique mistakes. They don't know the names of those you love, nor the things that give you sleepless nights. They won't have your talents or share your hobbies. They won't share your taste in music, books, TV series and films, or own the text messages you refuse to delete, or those that you did. They won't have the same psychological wounds as you, or know of the mini-celebrations you held, perhaps alone. They won't know how you question yourself, or share your take on faith. They won't know what you know – and what you don't. All this, and so much more. is what makes you unique, and this way of being unique, if properly channelled, always makes it possible for you to find love and goodness and to encounter others. There is no one like you, and sometimes we all need to remember Mendez's words in *The Butterfly Circus*: 'You are magnificent.'

The second quality is the opposite of the first: a serene humility. Why? In our uniqueness, we also have limitations and inconsistencies. We put our foot in it, we make mistakes, we sin. We do not always measure up to our dreams. Indeed, we may fall short of them. Sometimes we're surprised by our lack of vision, motivation or enthusiasm. We realise we are burying our talents because we feel insecure and mediocre. We need to recognise all this, without shying away, but also without unnecessary drama. We need to accept our own fracture lines, our own feet of clay, and to correct what we can. Why? Accepting what we are does not mean giving up on what we may become. We need to trust and calmly acknowledge that great things may yet be sculpted out of us, these vessels of clay.

Thirdly, we need to value our creativity: we are geniuses, we are creators. We have the ability to create new things in music or art, literature or science. How much progress has gestated in the solitude of a laboratory, a bedroom, a library or on a solitary walk! How many marvels of the modern world began with a lightbulb moment as someone had a flash of inspiration? How many discoveries have seen the light of day because someone had the courage to fight for their dreams?

We're capable of dreaming of futures that do not yet exist, of turning a blank canvas into a riot of colour. History provides us with countless examples of people much admired for their creativity. Think of Michelangelo before the ceiling of the Sistine Chapel. The canvas was already there, in the stone. What he, being a genius, did was to imagine what others could not see and express this. Exactly the same is true of so many others, whether architects transforming physical space, or scientists foreseeing a discovery. Or a sculptor carving out of stone the figure that was already there but which only they could sense. Or the storyteller whose imagination breathes life into characters. Or the poet who turns words into powerful written verse. Or the researcher, pursuing through years of constant labour, the cure for an illness.

There is a wonderful scene in the film *Begin Again* which helps us to understand this. Gretta is a young composer living in New York, her heart broken by her boyfriend leaving her. One day, in a bar, she's asked to sing. She gets up on stage with her guitar and begins. No one pays her much attention. People carry on doing their own thing: chatting, drinking, being noisy. In the midst of the racket, Gretta, singing about her broken heart, cannot be heard. However, someone is listening: Dan, a music producer, is the only person really listening to her. But he's not just listening to what he can hear in the bar. He goes further. In a fascinating scene, we get a glimpse of what Dan is seeing, and we hear what he's hearing: the musical arrangements that he is sensing might work with Gretta's song. All this goes way beyond what most people in the bar perceive. The arrangement of the song Dan imagines is full of possibility. Dan is an example of what creativity is. He reminds us that some people are just able to see life differently.[31]

The imagination is another faculty that allows our lives to become our heart song. We're able to imagine what we haven't seen, to dream of places we've never visited, and travel in our minds, guided, by words we're reading for the first time, to exotic, far-off places. Reading is like a door that transports us into other worlds. Unfortunately some people don't like reading. What a huge loss! I always say while there are books, there's hope, because books express our dreams and disappointments. Books are instructive: they introduce us to emotions, errors and discoveries, perhaps because there's a bit of an island in all of us. If we pool our words, our memories and our history we have a

---

31. A. Bregman and J. Apatow (producers) and J. Carney (director), *Begin Again*, Exclusive Media (2013), http://bit.ly/2xcB6pZ.

huge chance of growing and continuing the creative work that is our legacy. Imagination, knowledge, quests – all unfurl within the pages of the vast library of the history of humanity, in novels or essays, fiction or factual books, works of science or philosophy. We pour our deepest desires, our most daring fantasies and starkest truths into our books.

The reader is lent the words of the author, makes them their own and then takes off to navigate other worlds. Thanks to books, we may discover what it feels like to row a boat alone, or else to live as a guard, poet or prisoner: we may realise that each of us has a unique understanding of our country. We may solve mysteries, or travel at the speed of light, and see all the horror and all the beauty of the world. We may imagine being pacifists or soldiers, magicians or friars, live in the court of the Sun King or build medieval cathedrals. We may cross deserts and mountains, or journey through the streets of every city in the world. We may believe or doubt.

So, open a book, meander through the pages while your imagination soars. Use your imagination to colour in the scenes, the shadows and light, the odours, the appearance of each character. All this is another kind of heart song to be enjoyed alone.

Pity those who, out of ignorance, make the innocent boast, 'I don't like reading', because, perhaps without realising it, they have closed the door on exploring a thousand potential worlds. Several years ago, the following story appeared in the press: in Itápolis, a state of São Paulo in Brazil, books began to vanish from the local lending library, until the police discovered that a teenager was stealing them. He had 384 books – some stolen from other libraries too – at home, all kept in perfect order. He'd read them all. What motivated him was a passionate desire to learn and educate himself. An introvert by nature, he had taken the books fuelled by a desperate need to possess them. He was poor. 'He did this so as not to be out in the street,' his sister said. 'I was going to return the books some day,' he confessed.[32]

---

32. *El País*, 28 July 2017: http://bit.ly/2u4NnXj.

It is believable. Imagine this crazy young lad who chose to read, to dream, to travel with his imagination through a world he was otherwise, in all probability, excluded from. Imagine the passion with which, during those endless hours of reading, he savoured the words, gently touching the pages. Picture the light shining in his eyes as he discovered something new, or intuited the existence of exotic landscapes, characters and unfamiliar lives. We should be grateful to this young Brazilian because he reminds us that words are also a luxury, and reading a privilege, and the imagination a miracle.

Finally, leading on from this last point, it seems to me that we don't place enough value on our ability to reflect. Yet this is such an important part of life. Perhaps the reason is that today we place far more value on emotion, immediacy, feeling and passion. Perhaps we associate reflection with a kind of desiccated gaze, or a cold, bone-dry analysis of reality. Or perhaps it is because of a lazy but widespread opinion that decrees it pointless to really think things through. That's just not true. Our ability to reflect, to abstract, to draw our own conclusions, to analyse situations, values and desires is admirable. Reflection can address everything from the big existential questions to the minutiae of day-to-day life. We may ask questions about life and death and the meaning of what we do: Are there limits to science? Do consensual universal values exist? Are faith and reason compatible? Where will knowledge lead us? Is there a purpose to what we do or is everything just one big coincidence? How should our societies, politics and economies be organised? What is love? What is justice? We can devote our time and skill to reflecting on the big questions of life, the nature of reality, society and people. This ability is one of our greatest strengths. It's also probably one of our most solid reasons for affirming with hope that the future can be better, because there will always be someone capable of withstanding criticism and suggesting a better way forward. We are reflective by nature – or at least we have the ability to be so.

Everything I have mentioned above – taking pride in oneself and humility, the creativity we nurture by looking at the world and our

Part Four

capacity to reflect on life – are sometimes grouped under one heading: 'the interior life'. Yet this interior life is not merely a personal meditation on the events of existence. It may also take the form of spiritual life and, if we have faith, may provide the space for the ultimate encounter: with God.

18

The Interior Life: Is There Anyone out There?

We all have an interior life. We all devote time to thinking – sometimes consciously, at other times unconsciously. We all fantasise occasionally about life, letting our imagination flow as we oscillate between being aware of our own dignity and insecure about who we are. Our interior life doesn't happen in a void. It is replete with experiences, other people, our memories, feelings, words, sensations, the places and spaces we occupy.

However, it's worth highlighting at least one last dimension of our interior world that is universal, although we may all respond to it in different ways: the quest for faith and how we experience it. This includes questions about the meaning of life, our thirst for transcendence, and our vague longing for something or someone more. This sense, which is both question and quest, is part of the human condition and has been manifest throughout the history of every people, culture and age. It is not merely the vestige of a superstitious or irrational age, as some seem to assume today. The religious question is as alive today as ever. In our world, there are thousands of millions of believers on every latitude and in every situation. Some countries are without doubt more secularised than others, but even there that does not mean that the search for God is dead.

We question things. And we share the heart song of the faith which comes to us through our tradition, the experiences to which others have put a name and made our heritage. These experiences point towards the existence of God. We ponder eternity because we are finite, and we have questions too about transcendence, that state beyond death which we struggle so much to understand.

Faith has limitations. Yet we say faith is a gift, one developed through a combination of our upbringing and character, our appetite for leaping into the dark and taking a risk, our level of trust, and our acceptance that the universe is too big for us alone.

What is key is that as our own faith takes shape in line with the main religious instruction and formation we follow or receive, we open up a space within us to experience faith as an encounter with the divine. From my perspective as a Christian and, more specifically, a Catholic, I would like to suggest at least four places where such encounters may occur. The first is the world; the second, the Word; the third, the celebration of the sacraments, which have a powerful impact on the fundamental areas of life; and, lastly, personal prayer.

We discover God in the world. Many of the images (except within strictly theological contexts) we use to speak of God and about faith come from daily life. We describe God as a father or mother, a lover, a potter, a vine grower, or wisdom. We speak of others as our neighbours or brothers or sisters. We suggest that compassion, mercy, justice, goodness or beauty are traits of God. What are these words if not images taken from daily life which are reflections of the true nature of God? They teach us to see the world with the eyes of a believer, to name through faith many of the events that happen to us. Real life becomes the setting for a divine encounter the moment that the events in our lives become a sign pointing to the afterlife.

Sceptical philosophers claim that what believers do is take the best in people and project this onto our concept of a non-existent God. What if the reverse is true? What if what we really do is recognise God in the world around us? What if what is described as 'the best in people' is in fact a reflection of God latent in the core of reality? What if 'the best in people' is actually the seed of the spirit living within us? What if, in fact, God is the supreme example of the love that we may see in people who love passionately and with self-giving to the point of sacrificing their lives for others? What if the world, creation, good people and everything that surrounds us are divine clues pointing towards the existence of God?

Listening to the Word of God is another space for divine encounter. Why? In in this Word, made clear through centuries of scholarship and the witness and life of various peoples and exemplary individuals, the life of a specific figure is portrayed. The story is the history of salvation. The figure is Jesus Christ, the human face of God and the ultimate divine image of the human being. Listening to his Word means an experience of welcome, reflection and learning.

One of the great losses in the lives of many Christians is the Bible, which we neither know nor understand nor grasp how to read without sliding into fundamentalism. Yet we declare that through this extraordinary collection of books, written over the centuries and assembling the experience of eyewitnesses, we may gradually discover who and what God is, and what our lives might be. There we have both a challenge and an opportunity: to learn how to read the Bible as if it is addressed to each one of us individually, to grasp that its stories speak to our own lives and to sense that God is behind this. This is another heart song, which readies us to transform our lives into a graceful dance.

Very often liturgical celebrations don't mean anything to people; they have become an empty ritual that we don't understand, which doesn't relate to everyday life and which we attend as spectators rather than participants. Yet when we learn how to invest our lives in the sacraments and we realise how the various sacraments are about celebrating hope, new beginnings, the freedom of faith, the sharing of a common table, fraternity, love, forgiveness or death, and when we discover how this brings us into relationship with God, then once again, the Mass has meaning. And that's when the liturgy becomes a dance for the soul.

On the subject of prayer, we each learn to pray in different ways, to give meaning and purpose to what we do. Do we pray to feel we aren't alone? Is prayer a way of speaking to God? Does he listen to us? Do we hear him? Do we respond? Or not? To each of these questions, there are so many replies that whole books could be written on the many types of prayer and ways to pray. But I'd like to simply point out that whatever method or type of prayer we choose, what we're doing is reaching out to God, consciously opening a doorway to make manifest through faith our belief that God exists and hears us.

I've always been struck by one of Jesus' final lamentations on the Cross: 'My God, My God, why have you abandoned me?' He cries out in desperation, feeling condemned and using his last dregs of energy. Although I know that this is the start of a psalm, for a long time I thought that during this moment of greatest darkness for Jesus, even his Father had vanished from view. I felt overwhelmed, imagining that solitude and despair, that void, and how he felt abandoned at the moment of death. Years ago I understood that this was not so. It was not easy to understand, nonetheless.

When I was twenty years old, I became great friends with a fellow Jesuit whom I met in formation. He was called Isidore and he was twenty-two. He was a delightful person, deep and warm-hearted. Through the circumstances of our formation, we ended up living together for a year when we were both a bit disconnected from our year group. Due to this, we began to spend quite a lot of time together. We went to class together, and we spent our free time together. We challenged each other to games of ping-pong or played card games as a team (something that automatically creates a bond). Isidore loved writing. Sometimes he let me read his poems. I was impressed by his faith. Our days ended with a nocturnal stroll through the chill of Salamanca, as we chatted about life, our families, our faith, our vocations, and about the future – what it would look like, where we would be. We often had a laugh. We shared a lot as we got to know each other and settled into a deep friendship. The following year, Isidore was sent to Madrid. We kept in contact. Over Christmas he came with his community to spend a few days in Salamanca. We had lost nothing of our bond or the complicity of the previous year. We enjoyed a few days of happiness. On the last day of his visit we played a game of racquetball, just like the many we'd played together in the past. When this ended, Isidore mentioned that he was very tired, more so than normal.

On returning to Madrid, he still felt tired. He had to go to the doctor and was diagnosed with leukaemia. For months, he endured exhausting medical treatment. That August I was going to a work camp in Albania. I spent July in Madrid with Isidore's mother and two Jesuit friends. We took turns to be with Isidore in hospital. It was 1992. When I went to Albania, the last thing I said to Isidore, joking with him as always was, 'Behave yourself!' A few days later, I heard that he had just passed away.

I hadn't at any point wanted to believe he might die, and I wasn't ready to hear the news.

For months, from that moment on, I couldn't pray. The only word that came to mind when I sat in the chapel was an insistent 'Why?' That question was filled with rage, incomprehension, rebellion and denial. Which is why I felt that God could not possibly be present in my prayer.

However, as the weeks went by I began to realise something. In that 'Why?' there was more truth, honesty and authenticity than in many other pious words I had uttered at other times. There was also rage, pain and a sense of impotence. I began to realise that I wasn't really expecting an answer. I wasn't even angry with God. I knew that life was like this, although it was painful. However, in my rage, my letting it all out, my uncertainty, I had turned towards the one person towards whom, in that moment, I felt I could pour out my pain.

That's when I understood that when Jesus cries out from the Cross he does not do so out of fear of having lost God. What he is uttering is his last prayer, the only one he can possibly say at that point. A prayer born of sorrow, fear, the feeling of failure.

This is something which for me is the key to prayer. We speak to God from the place we're at, whether we're happy or our hearts are shrivelled, in gratitude when things are going well or out of frustration when we don't fulfil our dreams, whether we feel certain of our faith or doubtful. But the truth, which we know at times intuitively, is that however we are, God is always present, waiting for us on the other side of our prayer.

Conclusion

Two Final Images: Battle Scars and Borders

We are reaching the end of the journey. In the previous pages I have tried to reflect on loneliness and encounter, and about the silence that sometimes overwhelms us when loneliness is painful. I've also reflected on the instructive heart song that guides our steps into dancing with loneliness. This is a melody that rises to the surface of our consciousness from our fragility, containing the names of those we love most deeply, and the wisdom rooted in love and hardship that we acquire with others. It also comes from the doubts that trouble us and the faith which, in a bewildering balance of questions and certainties, opens us up to a remarkable future.

In the end, perhaps the most audacious and, at the same time, most obvious thing we can affirm is that we are not alone, although it may feel like it at times. We are not alone because every life is connected to other lives, through relationships replete with possibility and places where encountering others is possible. We bond with each other, we love each other, we seek each other, we disappoint and indulge each other. We look at each other constantly, sometimes with distrust, at other times in hope. We are as zealous and enthused about our own life journey as we are about the life journeys of the people we love most. In calm and lucid moments, we identify with each other as, looking at each other, we realise we are all made of the same clay, being in equal measure cracked and full of beauty.

I don't believe any lives are more interesting than others. All lives, without exception, are tales worth telling. Each life contains instances of heroism, unforgettable moments, caresses bestowed – or refused – borrowed words, dreams that come true, and others that exist only in our imagination. Every life is always different and unique, a tapestry woven with threads of love and care, excitement and anxiety, where plans fulfilled are stitched in gold while others are left half finished. There are heroes and villains, adventures and mundane routines, failures and victories, storm-filled nights and sunny days. Every life, with its crossroads and turmoil, triumphs and errors and the names of those engraved in its heart, deserves, at least once, to be celebrated. It's just that at times we simply can't find the words for this.

Human relationships are, naturally, both our strength and our weakness because they are what we pour our hearts and the very best of ourselves into. However, relationships can also reveal our mean-spiritedness and poverty of spirit. Should this weakness lead us to protect ourselves by hiding our heads in the clouds? Should we never allow anyone to come too close to our private space or our dreams and disappointments in case they might occasionally let us down or hurt us? I don't think so. There is no alternative to encounter. We are a family, a community, a tribe, a village.

In other words, we're arriving at the end of the journey having already shared a great deal but with much still to say. Almost certainly, some scars from the past may have, by this point in our journey, come to the fore. To be honest, this should never worry us. What we should worry about is reaching the end of our lives untouched, in pristine condition, instead of being exhausted from intensely engaging with life, body and soul. Our scars are physical and internal, spiritual, psychological and emotional … because all of that comprises who we are. This core is where we hold the names of those we have lost, next to those we have loved but, for whatever reason, lost; the battles we had to fight, whether we emerged a loser or victorious; the words that once wounded others or that we said in haste and could not retract, which are indelibly etched in our hearts. Likewise, we are scarred by our illnesses and limitations, the conflicts we couldn't resolve, our experiences of rejection, our impossible dreams. But it is all worth it. The real tragedy would be discovering, too late in the day, that we have merely lived like ghosts, barely interacting with the real world.

On the subject of wounds, I would like to mention a true story that has fascinated me since the first time I heard it. Silvia Abascal is a well-known Spanish actress who has starred since her youth in popular television series. Later in her career, she became well-known for her theatre and film work. After years of effort and struggling to find her place professionally, Abascal finally found stability in her career. She was enjoying that final moment between youth and maturity when opportunities were flooding her way from all directions. One night, quite unexpectedly, while she was on the jury of the Malaga cinema festival, just before the closing party, she had a stroke. From that day forward, a different chapter began in her life: illness, the need for surgery, and the discovery that skills which, only a day earlier, she had taken for granted would now be a daily battle. Forced to face all this, she found courage, refusing to give up or to indulge in self-pity. If she had to fight, so be it. She tells the story in a fascinating book, *Todo un Viaje*.[33]

One particular episode of her story comes across as a very personal experience. When Silvia had open brain surgery, she had to shave off part of her hair before the operation. The operation left her with an enormous scar across her skull. She wrote: 'That scar became for better or worse a "sensory cord". My boyfriend insisted on cleaning the scar every day. My treatment lasted more than three months. When he kissed my scar, time stood still. Seconds lasted for ever. That kiss was an instant connection to the deepest, most vulnerable part of me. And I received it as an infinite gesture of self-giving and of love.'[34]

At other points in the book, Abascal alludes to the importance of scars, and the silent message they emit in people's lives. This is what I would like to reflect on here. We all react differently when facing our scars. Whether external or internal, they show how vulnerable we are. They expose us, forcing us to acknowledge that we are fragile. They remind us of our wounds (some may still be painful). And perhaps one of the most universal of all temptations is to hide them. The fact they make us feel very insecure leads us to retreat with them in private.

In Abascal's situation, many people would have sought to protect themselves. A scar like that in the world of entertainment where image

---

33. S. Abascal, *Todo un Viaje,* Barcelona: Planeta, 2013.
34. Ibid., 79.

is all-important, could have become a real blight, a problem only magnified by illness and a slow recovery. However, that moment of intimacy that Abascal describes above tells a different story, exemplifying trust, tenderness, closeness and acceptance. Perhaps the bravest thing we can ever do is to reveal our deepest vulnerability to those with whom we reveal the full truth of who we are.

All of us, I believe, occasionally need someone to touch our scars with tenderness. This cannot be forced or demanded but neither should we take it for granted. It will occur in a relationship over time. It is won through friendship, in love, and through our capacity to open our hearts so that we may reach those who seek us, and find those we seek. Perhaps it is within our grasp to cultivate the ability to be tender, considerate and caring, so that when another person is deeply hurt they may feel safe and at home with us. We will also need at particular points in our life to trust someone else, allowing them to tell us, perhaps without words, that they support us, by gently kissing or caressing our wounds.

As well as scars, another image always comes to mind whenever I think of loneliness: borders. Latterly they've had a very bad press, because they're becoming ever more a place of separation and of exclusion. Borders are, all too often, a wired electric fence, an obstacle or natural barrier capable of killing anyone who is fleeing for their lives. A frontier may be a real wall or an imaginary one. A frontier is what separates 'us' from 'them', what divides the world into 'my people' and others. The more cut off we want to be, the more frontiers we erect. Europe appears to be determined to restore exclusion and national boundaries to the point where the dream of a united Europe is dying because the United Kingdom is refusing to keep its borders open. Elsewhere, electoral campaigns toy with the public's fears about national security by strengthening borders until no one may cross them. It certainly seems as though national frontiers are the ultimate borders, which we cannot or should not cross.

However, I think that frontiers are also – or could be – just the reverse: a place to meet, a place where, if we're not afraid of each other and if we don't reject each other, we could meet to discuss what makes us different. For centuries, many border posts became enclaves where cities belonging to two countries proliferated. They were visited by citizens from both sides of the border, who were keen to swap goods, glimpse a culture unlike their own, and extend a toe into alien territory. From this perspective, a frontier may be a place of learning, of mingling and of mutual enrichment.

I believe the first frontier we encounter is each one of us. We ourselves are the first boundary with other people. We may become a place of separation or of meeting, of exclusion or openness. We may hide ourselves within invisible armour that isolates us from others, or we may take the risk of togetherness and interacting or dancing with others. Yes, each of us is definitely both a frontier and meeting point, a barrier or a bridge to others, an isolated fort or an open house. And it is just here, through the way we resolve our dilemmas, that we hazard our ability to tango alone or together.

Frontiers

Where safety ends and fear begins,
There, just there, with your hand outstretched, ask me to cross over.

Where noise ends and loneliness begins,
There, just there, protect me with your words.

Where selfishness ends, and justice begins,
There, just there, compassion transforms my perspective.

Where nostalgia ends, and the future begins,
There, just there, is hope.

Where the wounds stop bleeding and the scars develop,
There, just there, is the tenderness which heals us.

Where memory fades and forgetfulness begins,
There, just there, is eternity, fending off ingratitude.

Where laughter dries up and the weeping starts,
There, just there is the consolation. And tears bring relief.

Where the party ends and routine returns,
There, just there, is your heart song.

Where night ends and day begins,
there, just there, is your dawn.

When strength goes and weakness sinks in,
There, just there, is the bread of blessing

When rage fades and peace begins,
There, just there, is your embrace.